SELECTED SPEECHES
VOLUME 2

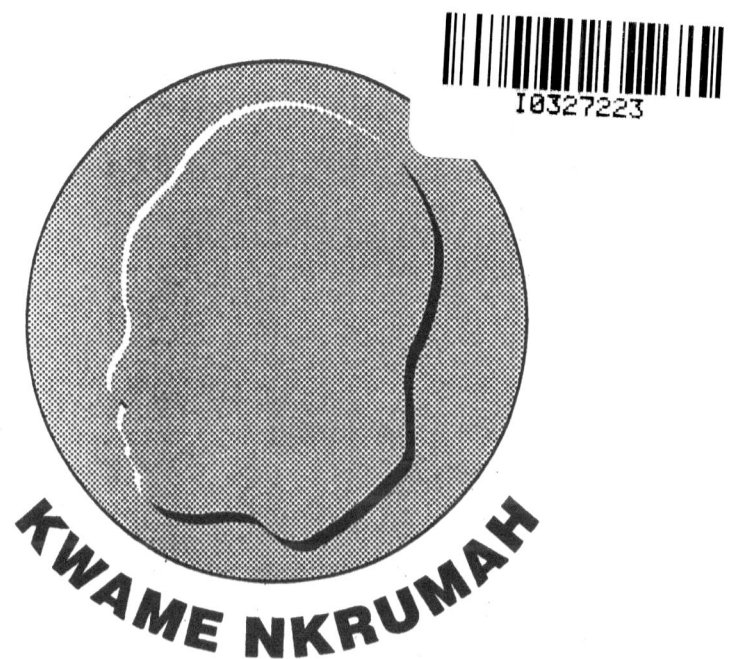

KWAME NKRUMAH

Compiled by Samuel Obeng

AFRAM PUBLICATIONS (GHANA) LTD.

Published by:

Afram Publications (Ghana) Ltd.,
P. O. Box M. 18,
Accra, Ghana,

© **The Republic of Ghana, 1960**

All Rights Reserved. No part of this book may be reprinted, or reproduced or utilized in any form or by any electronic, invented or other means, now known, including photocopying or recording, or any information storage and retrieval system, without permission in writing from Afram Publications (Ghana) Limited.

First Published 1979
This Edition 1997

ISBN 9964 70 202 7

Typeset by Damana Graphics

Printed by

FOREWORD

The death of Dr. Kwame Nkrumah, first President of the Republic of Ghana, on April 27, 1972, demonstrated one of the great ironies of our time. That a man who was so much maligned, condemned and rejected by his own people should at his death be praised and loved so much and be finally accepted by his own people again, appears to testify to Nkrumah's charisma.

Not even those he antagonised by the severity of some of his actions during his life-time could deny that by his death Kwame Nkrumah became the victor. The fact that he died so far away from home and away from the people he had loved so much, as well as the long, painful suffering he had to undergo before his death, could in a sense be regarded as his purgation. Nkrumah's death should transcend all feelings of hatred, animosity and revenge and should enjoin Ghanaians and freedom lovers everywhere to live in a spirit of reconciliation and brotherly love.

Many tributes have already been paid to Kwame Nkrumah by several Heads of State and Governments, distinguished individuals, politicians and church leaders all over the world. All these tributes have one common denominator—the greatness of the man. This is the quality of this great African which runs through this collection of speeches.

Nkrumah's speeches, some of which are being presented together to the world for the first time in this collection. still glow with the force of his personality, his conviction in the face of powerful opposition, his originality, his vision as well as his impatience.

Kwame Nkrumah brought freedom and unity to Ghana and it was his dream to unite the whole continent of Africa in freedom, and bring dignity to the African in his own land. But while he worked relentlessly towards this end, his methods and sometimes his priorities were not always easily accepted by all. On his death, many proclaimed Nkrumah's strategy.

To Kwame Nkrumah, Ghana's independence was only meaningful when the whole of the continent was also independent. To some this was an extravagant claim; but events in Africa today have demonstrated the wisdom and the foresight of the stand taken in his life time. Nkrumah did not live to see all his dreams realised; but in these speeches and in his writings he has left for posterity ideas which should inspire Africans and Black people everywhere.

Kwame Nkrumah realised that in a continental unity, Africa's vast natural and mineral potential could be better harnessed in such a manner as to hasten the economic and industrial development of the continent. Nkrumah believed that Africa can only be developed .md emancipated by Africans themselves and that no foreign power could claim to have an altruistic interest in the continent. Nkrumah also stressed that Africans should rely upon themselves for their own development instead of running about cap in hand after foreign assistance.

Nkrumah believed in the welfare of the common man. He was a friend of the workers and worked hard to build a strong Trades Union Congress in Ghana.

His speeches which relate to agriculture show how much Kwame Nkrumah did for Ghana in this field. At Kpandu in January, 1960, he stressed the importance of agriculture as Ghana's "basic industry" and the Government's policy to devote increasing, attention to it. Consequently, Ghana's Five-Year Development Plan concentrated on the diversification of agriculture. This is indeed the cornerstone of Ghana's economic development. What went wrong with Nkrumah's programme was the absence of proper machinery to ensure follow up action. The various farms which were established under Kwame Nkrumah are still an important source of food for Ghanaians.

Under Kwame Nkrumah, Ghana made significant advances in infrastructural development, especially, in the field of education, health, housing, and telecommunication. Tema Harbour and the Volta project remain living monuments to his dedication to serve the interests of the people.

Kwame Nkrumah did not confine his energies to the development and progress of Ghana. He played an important part in world affairs. Ironically, however, he was on a peace mission to Hanoi when he lost his Government. As one of the architects of non-alignment, Kwame Nkrumah was recently honoured in Georgetown where plagues were unveiled to his memory and to the memory of his colleagues and fellow fighters namely, President Nasser of Egypt, President Tito of Yugoslavia and Prime Minister Nehru of India.

Nkrumah is no more; but the ideas which impregnated his life and which are enshrined in these speeches will never die.

COL. I. K. ACHEAMPONG

Head of State and Chairman of the Supreme Military Council

PREFACE

Osagyefo Dr. Kwame Nkrumah had always been in the vanguard of what he himself called "The African Revolution." He had not only been at the centre of its political action, but had also articulated its ideology.

After Dr. Nkrumah's Government was overthrown by a military coup d' etat, on February 24, 1966, he was so much maligned, condemned and rejected by his own people that his books, speeches and pictures that could be reached were publicly burnt.

One afternoon in August, 1971 when I heard a news broadcast on Ghana Broadcasting Corporation Radio that an Act 380 of 28th August, 1971, had banned the use of any slogan by word or shiboleth, photograph, or policy document intended to revive the Convention People's Party (CPP) or its leader or chairman Dr. Kwame Nkrumah, I decided to gather the speeches from those who had them.

I wrote to the Government of the National Redemption Council when the obnoxious Act 380 of August, 1971 was repealed by NRCD 21 of 9th February, 1972, and was given a written permission to compile and publish the Speeches of Kwame Nkrumah.

Kwame Nkrumah's speeches, most of which are being presented together to the world in these volumes, still glow with the force of his personality, his conviction in the face of powerful opposition, his originality, his vision as well as his impatience when his expectations seemed delaying.

Nkrumah did not live to see all his dreams realised, but in his speeches and writings, he has left for posterity ideas which should inspire Africans and Black people everywhere.

It is my hope that readers of these volumes and future generations will derive from these pages the inspiration to fight to uproot the remnants of colonialism from the society.

Samuel Obeng
Compiler

Kumasi,
August, 1997

Dedicated to
Politicians and Ex-servicemen
and Brothers and Sisters in the Diaspora
who laid down their lives
to make Ghana's Independence possible

"Truth forever on the scaffold,
Wrong forever on the throne
Yet that scaffold sways the future,
And, behind the dim unknown,
Standeth God within the shadow,
Keeping watch above his own."

—James Russel Lowell

CONTENTS

1. Casablanca Conference..1
2. The Kwame Nkrumah Institute......................................5
3. Death of Patrice Lumumba...15
4. The Volta River Project..28
5. The Visit of Josip Broz-Tito...42
6. On Department from Commonwealth Leaders Conference..........49
7. On His Return to Ghana..51
8. Noble Task of Teaching..54
9. Dawn Broadcast...58
10. Africa Must Be Free..67
11. Building a Socialist State..69
12. The Fight on Two Fronts...83
13. Politics are not for Soldiers...96
14. Tragedy in Angola...98
15. New Horizons..113
16. The CPP 12th Anniversary..121
17. Padmore The Missionary...124
18. Work For Ghana And The Future..............................127
19. The Voice Of Africa..135
20. Flower of Learning (1)..138
21. Strengthening The Bonds Of Industry.......................148
22. Flower of Learning (2)..151
23. Christmas Broadcast..158
24. A Christmas Toast At A Dinner For Ambassadors And Ministers..168
25. Season of Goodwill...170

1

CASABLANCA CONFERENCE

Casablanca
January 7, 1961

YOUR MAJESTY, YOUR EXCELLENCIES,

It is with deep satisfaction that I make a few remarks on the general business of the conference. In fact my heart is filled with boundless joy for the great success which, in my view, has attended our efforts at this meeting. This beautiful Casablanca has known another meeting of Heads of State with a difference. This is a meeting of African Heads of African States for the discussion of African affairs in the interest of African peoples, and it is therefore unique, for it constitutes a prodigious and revolutionary challenge to the colonial powers and indeed the whole world in relation to its attitude towards Africa.

For six days we have sat here and thought and argued and argued only to agree in the end. This has given an irrefutable evidence that African leaders are capable of taking charge of their own African affairs and problems. I am proud to say that I have lived to see this day when the history of Africa is being made and the foundation laid for African Unity and solidarity by Africans.

When I received the invitation from His Majesty to attend this meeting, I was conceiving a conference of this nature myself. However, my thoughts flashed back to my first visit to Morocco in 1958 when after the Accra Conference of Independent African States I was touring the then only eight African Independent States on our continent. I was overwhelmed with a recollection of many pleasant memories of His Majesty's effusive hospitality. I know, of course, that this time even though I would meet the same typical Moroccan hospitality, I would also have to sit around the Conference table and thereby mix this remarkable hospitality with the anxiety of work. These past few days have proved me right, for I have had the pleasure, indeed all of us have the great pleasure of a wonderful reception, but also we have had to endure a great deal of work in order to achieve the results we have achieved.

Within a short period of time, we have discussed the Congo, which is the main subject of this Conference, but we have also covered subjects of great importance to Africa, and in all these matters our meeting has shown a great sense of responsibility and a determination to succeed in our purpose. I have no doubt that the leaders who have met at this Conference are all great nationalists of no mean order, we have demonstrated unmistakably to the whole world in various ways their iron opposition to colonialism and imperialism and their granite resolve to liquidate these evils from the face of our beloved continent.

For my part, I must say that as long as I live, and as long as any little vestige of colonialism and imperialism remains in Africa, I shall prosecute a ruthless war on these monsters, a war in which there shall be no truce. Colonialism and imperialism have no honour, no shame, no morals and conscience. The devastation which they have wrought in Africa is without parallel anywhere in the history of the world, but now Africans have arrived on the scene. We have arrested their progress and are determined to give them battle with all the forces at our command until we have achieved the total liberation of the African Continent and have built a strong Union of African States. As I have always stated, and as I will continue to proclaim, I can see no security for African States unless African leaders like ourselves have realized beyond all doubts that salvation for Africa lies in Unity.

Your Majesty, Excellencies, let us unite, for in unity lies strength, and as I see it, African states must unite or sell themselves out to imperialist and colonialist exploiters for a mess of pottage, or disintegrate individually.

The future of Africa lies in a political union—a political union in which the economic, military and cultural activities will be co-ordinated for the security of the continent. The land of Africa is so compact in its geographical entity that there should be very little obstacle in the way of the creation of the Union of African States.

I know of course that the colonialists and imperialists are greatly disturbed and most unhappy about our talk on African Unity. They are not going to sit down with folded arms. So through their press, radio and other means of propaganda they peddle every lie and slander to incite jealously and hate among African leaders. But we must not allow them to succeed. The objectives before us are so precious and all-important that the thought of them alone must fortify and continue to unite us in the pursuit of these glorious objectives.

What I fear worst of all is the fact that if we do not formulate plans for unity and take active steps to form a political union, we would soon be fighting and warring among ourselves with imperialists and colonialists standing behind the screen and pulling vicious wires, to make us cut each other's throat for the sake of their diabolical purposes in Africa. All over Africa artificial boundaries dividing brother from brother, sister from sister have been erected by the colonizers. It is within the greater context of African Union that these artificial boundaries imposed by colonialism and imperialism will disappear.

I must state here that the presence of the Representative of Ceylon has given me great pleasure indeed, for it has given concrete proof of Afro-Asian solidarity which is one of the things the imperialists and colonialists fear most of all. I would like therefore to congratulate Her Excellency the Prime Minister of Ceylon and to wish Ceylon great success in her endeavour to undo the evils of colonialism in their country. It is only right that I should congratulate personally the Ceylon Representative here at this meeting who has contributed so much to the success of our deliberations.

Your Majesty, I hope you will allow me to say how much I appreciate your kindness and your great hospitality to us whilst we have been here. This beautiful city of Casablanca has a unique air of restfulness about it which enables hard work, much as we have been through, to be endured with pleasantness.

On behalf of my own self and my delegation, and on behalf of my brother leaders who have been here with me at your invitation, I wish to convey to you an expression of our warmest thanks for your distinguished hospitality. We shall take away the most pleasant memories of your country, and shall look forward to returning again to this historic city. I hope that it will be possible for Your Majesty also to visit Ghana in the near future so that we may be able to repay in a very small degree the debt of gratitude which we owe to Your Majesty.

I wish to assure my brother Heads of State here that the decisions which have been taken at this Conference will no doubt receive the ratification of the Ghana Parliament which, I know, will readily give legislative backing to the moral obligations contained in these decisions.

Now that the blazing fire of African nationalism sweeps everything before it in our continent; now that the imperialists quake and shiver in spite of their intrigues and machinations to retain their nefarious position in Africa, let us re-double our efforts. Let us determine more than ever before to crush colonialism and imperialism from the face of our beautiful Africa.

Again, Your Majesty, I thank you very much and trust that Providence will spare you long enough to see this struggle to a victorious end.

2

THE KWAME NKRUMAH INSTITUTE

LAYING OF THE FOUNDATION STONE OF AND THE INAUGURATION OF THE FIRST COURSE OF THE IDEOLOGICAL SECTION OF THE INSTITUTE

Winneba
February 18, 1961

COMRADES AND FRIENDS,

This day is historic. It is historic because it is the positive beginning of the end of reaction in Ghana through conscious ideological education. It is also historic for another reason. At this meeting of our party today, we have with us a distinguished visitor–one of the illustrious sons of the Union of Soviet Socialist Republics, Mr. Leonid Ilyich Brezhnev, President of the Praesidium of the Union of Soviet Socialist Republics. The President accepted an invitation from me to visit Ghana at the end of his visit to Guinea. I feel sure that the friendship between our two countries will be strengthened by this visit.

As many of you do know, the circumstances of the Convention People's Party, the victorious party of Gold Coast revolution, made it practically impossible to organise any consistent party ideological education. Our party was in death-grips with imperialism and colonialism, and it was a grim fight every inch of the way. The objective of independence was so precious that everything else, including party ideological education, had to be pushed aside in the interim. Thus it has been, that apart from some patch-up nationalist political education, no serious effort for ideological education has previously been undertaken by the Convention People's Party.

The great political struggle which the party started in 1949 formally ended in 1957, when independence was achieved. To the leadership of the party this great struggle did not end until the 1st of July, 1960, when the people of Ghana appointed for themselves the means of government by drawing up a constitution of their own.

For twelve years, twelve long years, therefore, no conscious, consistent effort had been made to provide party members with the requisite education in the party's ideology of socialism—socialism based on the conditions, circumstances and peculiarities of our African life.

Today, this unsatisfactory state of affairs comes to an end by the establishment of this institute, which the Central Committee names the Kwame Nkrumah Institute, here at Winneba, to give to the membership of our dynamic party not only the necessary education which should prepare it for the successful prosecution of the difficult task of our social, economic, industrial and technological reconstruction, but also the victorious pursuit of the struggle for African freedom and unity and the complete and total liquidation of colonialism.

At this moment, my mind is thrown back to the day—the remarkable 9th of December, 1947—when I again set foot on the soil of the land of my birth after my wanderings abroad in search of the Golden Fleece.

It is unnecessary to repeat here in detail what I have already set down in writing in my autobiography. Nevertheless it is right, in my opinion, to recapitulate some of the basic sign-posts marking the land which the Convention People's Party has covered in victory and in defeat during these twelve years of active national struggle.

As you all know I arrived at the instance of the Working Committee of the United Gold Coast Convention and immediately plunged into organisational work—work absolutely essential for mobilising our people against the weight of British imperial might in the Gold Coast.

Then followed rapidly the 1948 boycott of goods, the cowardly shooting of ex-servicemen at the Osu cross-roads, the disturbances and the detention of the men, including myself, who were supposed to have planned these national disorders.

Comrades, these reminiscences are like tonic to my soul; I cast my eyes back across the field of struggle and see the historic landmarks telling the story of progress which has covered the trail of the Convention People's Party.

I see myself before the Watson Commissioners. I see again the slacking in effect of the leaders of the United Gold Coast Convention. I form the Committee on Youth Organisation to ginger up activities of the United Gold Coast Convention. It evokes jealousies and misunderstandings. I am dismissed from my post. The masses rebel against the leadership of the Convention. I stand at the reconciliation meeting at Saltpond. Our ideas are poles apart. I resign. The youth breaks away from the movement. I form the Convention People's Party, on June 12, 1949.

The Convention People's Party took up the struggle in real earnest. Then came the Coussey Committee and their half-hearted recommendations for constitutional reform with which the Convention People's Party violently disagreed.

The Party demanded Self-Government now, with the slogan "we prefer self-government with danger to servitude in tranquility," and pushed the backs of the imperialists against the wall.

Persecution started and liable suits were filed against me for claims running into thousands of pounds. This was September, 1949. On January 8, 1950, I declared Positive Action, and was arrested on the 20th of January, 1950, tried and thrown into prison, in accordance with the super-excellent tenets of colonial justice which colonialists invariable mete out to their colonial subjects who dare to question their right to oppress people.

Comrades, we have come a long way up the road since then.

I can hear once again the singing of the masses in the evenings outside the prison walls. I can feel once more the violent throbbing of my heart as the blood of inspiration runs through my veins and steels my nerves for the tough struggle ahead. I can see how the party comrades toiled day and night to keep the party flag flying in those days of severe trails.

Then followed the series of our party election victories, my release from prison walls. on the 20th February, 1951 and the formation of the first Government of the Convention People's Party in 1951.

Why do I recount these matters? Why am I re-living the past? Why have I to remind the country of these historical facts?

Comrades, I do so because we have reached a point in the life of our nation when it is absolutely necessary to recapture the lofty spirit of our past and bring home vividly to all members of the Convention People's Party that the end result of the national task is not individual gain and personal prosperity but service to the country and the masses for the cultivation of popular prosperity. The free development of each should be the conclusion for the free development of all.

The road of the struggle led on and on. The party convened the Gold Coast Representative Assembly. We threw our historic challenge to our opponents to join us in declaring another positive action. They recoiled into their conspiratorial dens. We went forward from one sign-post to another until the 10th of July, 1953, when I tabled the "Motion of Destiny" in the Legislative Assembly and called on Britain to hand over power to the people themselves.

The sweeping victory of our party in the 1954 general elections followed. We were seated firmly in the saddle, moving steadily on to our goal.

But the imperialists and colonialists were not sleeping. They worked fast with opponents, and produced the National Liberation Movement, which exerted itself to wreck everything the nation had gained so far and bring back colonialism again upon the people. They attempted exactly what they are now enacting in the Congo, and very soon possibly in Angola. Thanks to the solidarity and strength of our dynamic party, we pulled through what would otherwise have spelled national disaster and engendered despair and failure.

We moved forward again to 1956, obtained another resounding victory over the forces of reaction and sabotage in the imposed general elections, and finally cleared the way for the ushering in of independence and sovereignty on the 6th of March, 1957.

The Convention People's Party moved on, always living up to its motto: "Forward ever, backward never." So on we went to the national plebiscite, and the residential elections, to give to ourselves a Constitution of our own making, creating Ghana a Republic on the 1st of July, 1960.

Comrades, I have looked back a little, looked over the period spanning the last twelve years, to see our performance in a nutshell, and I say "Well done" to the Convention People's Party.

The struggle still continues, but it continues on a different plane.

Now the Convention People's Party and the people of Ghana grapple with a different problem–the problem of social, cultural, scientific, economic, industrial and technological reconstruction, which must be solved expeditiously, thus repairing the damage done to our country by the imperialist and colonialist despoilers.

But is that the only remaining problem? Not by any means.

There is also the major problem of the total liberation of Africa and Union of African States.

From my days in London up to the present, I have never once stopped shouting to all Africa about African unity. The sad episode in the Congo more than justifies my fears the unwisdom to stand alone, each by itself, in the face of this fierce onslaught by the new colonialists, who are equally if not more dangerous and merciless in their come-back endeavours.

When, therefore, I have come to this town of Winneba to lay the foundation stone of the Kwame Nkrumah Institute and to inaugurate the first course in ideological training accommodated in temporary premises, I see a beam of hope shooting across our continent, for the things which will be taught in this institute will strengthen African youth and manhood and inspire it to scale great heights; and the men and women who will pass through this institute will go out not only armed with analytical knowledge to wage the battle of African socialism but will also be fortified with a keen spirit of dedication and service to our motherland.

This institute will comprise two sections, namely the Ideological education Training Centre and the Positive Action Training Centre.

Everyone of us, from members of the Central Committee, Ministers and high party officials, to the lowest propagandist in the field, will pass through a course in this institute for proper orientation and adjustment. Furthermore, the institute will provide training for non-violent positive actionists, Party Vanguard activists, farmers, co-operators, trade unionists, and women organisers, giving particular care to leadership training and making sure that a forum is provided for members of public corporations, the civil service and other governmental bodies for the discussion of the party's programmes, aims, and policies.

Hitherto, the Central Committee and I have viewed with leniency the mistakes of party comrades on the ground that the party had given them no ideological education. From now on, that excuse will not avail anyone who has passed through this institute and gone through the necessary course.

Hitherto, it has been true to say that many members of the Convention People's Party have not understood the significance and value of the membership. This will be corrected when they have passed through the Kwame Nkrumah Institute.

To any Ghanaian, membership of our party should rightly form the dearest possession. The Convention People's Party has been built with great sacrifice and endeavour, iron determination and outstanding patriotism, overwhelming nationalist zeal and selfless comradely service. It is the people's own party, rigidly dedicated to the cause and welfare of the whole people of Ghana and uncompromisingly devoted to a relentless fight against imperialism and colonialism found anywhere on the continent of Africa, or in the world, for that matter. No one can deny that the convention People's Party is thus pitchforked by historical circumstances into the spear-head and vanguard of the gigantic struggle for the total liberation of Africa and the independence and unity of African states.

Comrades, as you yourselves have seen, it is a great honour to belong to the fold of the Convention People's Party. But it is right to remind ourselves that this membership carries also a serious responsibility.

Members of the party must be the first to set an example of all the highest qualities in the nation. We must excel in our field of work by working really hard. We must produce unimpeachable evidence of integrity, honesty, selflessness and faithfulness in the positions in which we are placed by the party in service to the nation. We must eschew ridiculous ostentation and vanity when the party has charged us with eminent offices of state, and remember constantly that we hold such offices not in our own right of the total membership of the Convention People's Party, the masses of the people who really matter.

I must thus personally warn all members of the Central Committee, all party functionaries, all Ministers of State and Ministerial Secretaries, and chairmen of public boards and corporations and other key public officials, that they owe a great duty to the people—a duty which must be discharged with the highest sense of responsibility.

They must at all times feel conscious of the truth that in ourselves, all of us are nothing except what the party has made us—namely, agents for the execution of the party's programme. It is a travesty of trust, therefore, for anyone of us to consider that we are privileged to install ourselves as masters of the people instead of servants of the masses. The leaders of the party must forge a consistent band of brotherhood with the rank and file of the party, and build a living solidarity for the protection of the people's welfare and the realisation of our party objectives.

No comrades should pass through this institute and fail to go out with a proclamation on his lips saying: I have not for myself but for the good of the whole people. The socialist ideals which we pursue must imbue all who pass through this institute with a spirit of selfless devotion to the cause of the nation, to the cause of Africa, and to the cause of the world.

All members of the Convention People's Party who pass through this institute will have a great opportunity for broadening their political knowledge and ideological understanding. They will strengthen their qualities of loyalty and discipline, thereby increasing the overall discipline of the party and the deep affection and loyalty of the general membership.

The structure of the Convention People's Party has been built up from our own experiences, conditions, environments and concepts entirely Ghanaian and African in outlook, and based on the Marxist socialist philosophy and worldview.

Our party is likened to a tree—a huge and mighty tree with great branches sticking out everywhere. The trunk and the branches from the tree. It is a single unit, living a single life, and when it dies it dies a single death.

It would appear that many people are under the impression that the four great branches of the Convention People's Party, namely the Trades Union Congress, the United Ghana Farmers Council, the National Co-operative Council and the National Council of Ghana Woman, are mere affiliates of the Convention People's Party. They are not.

These four great wings of the party are not affiliates. They are a composite part of the Convention People's Party. That is to say they are integral elements of the party, living with it and dying with it, as a single entity.

It would be a good idea to qualify them for internal purposes as the Party Industrial Organisation, the Party Agricultural Organisation, the Party Co-operative Organisation and the Party Woman's Organisation. Members of these organisations must bear this position in mind in all their activities, and so must all other party members.

In addition to these four branch organisations there operates the National African Socialist Students Organisation–the NASSO.

This is the custodian body of the party's ideology and is composed of the most advanced ideological comrades torchbearers of the party's ideas and principles. The Nasso form the bark of this mighty tree, and cements the physical and organisational unity of the Convention People's Party.

This institute is, primarily, their school of action. They must be here day and night, imparting knowledge to their less favoured comrades who have not graduated to the NASSOist level.

They must make sure that the whole country is sprinkled with party study groups—yes, in the factories, workshops, departments and Ministries of Government, corporations, boards, and in every nook and corner of Ghana, there must exist a party study group, studying African socialism, party decisions, and programmes, explaining Government actions and policies and actively pursuing the "Cipipification" of the national life.

The Kwame Nkrumah Institute will not cater for Ghana alone. Its doors will be opened to all from Africa and the world both who seek knowledge to fit themselves for the great freedom fight against imperialism and colonialism old or new, and the consolidation of peace throughout the world for the progress of mankind.

I can envisage the future possibilities of this arrangement. When African freedom fighters from all over Africa have come into this institute and quenched their thirst for ideological knowledge, they will go back fortified in the same principles and beliefs, pursue the same objectives and aims, appreciate the same values and advocate the same themes. I see before my mind's eye a great monolithic party growing up out of this process, united and strong, spreading its protective wings over the whole of Africa—from Algiers in the north to Cape Town in the south; from Cape Guardafui in the east to Darkar in the west.

Comrades and friends, at this very moment Ghana mourns the death by brutal murder of Patrice Lumumba, late Prime Minister of the Congo, and his two associates Mpolo and Okito.

We at this gathering should do honour to their memory. But before I call for the observance of a two-minute silence, I wish to say this: Up to today, the murderers of Premier Lumumba and his two associates Mpolo and Okito, have been clouded in mystery.

The childish story of villagers killing these stalwart freedom fighters is the most absurd fabrication, that could emanate only from the diseased brains of Belgian colonialists and their puppet agents.

But just this very afternoon, it has been revealed to me by a reliable source that the murder of Patrice Lumumba, of Maurice Mpolo and of Joseph Okito took place on January 18th.

The information reveals that the men were sent for, one by one, and commanded to kneel and pray. Then, as he prayed, each was shot in the back by the order of a Belgian officer.

When Patrice Lumumba knelt to pray, the African soldier who was ordered to shoot him refused to do so, whereupon the Belgian officer took his revolver and shot Lumumba himself.

I have narrated these facts, not in any desire further to hurt your already wounded hearts. On the contrary, I have done so in order that you who pass through this institute, which I am proud to say bears my name, and which will stand forever for the principles and ideas for which I have always stood and eternally stand, may know the diabolical depths of degradation to which these twin-monsters of imperialism and colonialism can descend. You will then be able to assess the magnitude of the task still ahead and offer yourselves in sacrificial dedication to the cause of African freedom and unity.

Let us all stand up in silence for two minutes for our murdered brothers and comrades in arms.

And now, comrades and friends, first is my most pleasant duty to declare the foundation stone of the Kwame Nkrumah Institute well and truly laid. I feel happy to declare also the first course of the ideological training centre of the institute duly inaugurated.

Thank you.

3

DEATH OF PATRICE LUMUMBA

Accra
February 14, 1961

Countrymen, African Freedom Fighters, Comrades and Friends,

Somewhere in Katanga in the Congo—where and when we do not know—three of our brother freedom fighters have been done to death.

There have been killed Patrice Lumumba, the Prime Minister of the Republic of the Congo, Maurice Mpolo, the Minister in his Government who was elected from Katanga Province, and Joseph Okito, the Vice President of the Congolese Senate.

About their end many things are uncertain but one fact is crystal clear—they have been killed because the United Nations, whom Patrice Lumumba himself, as Prime Minister, had invited to the Congo to preserve law and order, not only failed to maintain that law and order, but also denied to the lawful Government of the Congo all other means of self-protection.

History records many occasions when rulers of States have been assassinated. The murder of Patrice Lumumba and of his two colleagues, however, is unique in that this is the first time in history that the legal ruler of a country has been done to death with the open connivance of a world organisation on whom that ruler put his trust.

These are the facts. Patrice Lumumba was appointed Prime Minister by the departing Belgian authorities because he was the leader of the Parliamentary Party with the largest representation and was the only Member of Parliament who could obtain a majority in both the Senate and the Chamber. Kasavubu was subsequently elected as the ceremonial Head of the State but it was clearly agreed and understood that he should have no more authority or power than has the King of the Belgians in Belgium. This fact, clearly written into the Constitution of the Congo, has been deliberately ignored and distorted by those who have sought for their own ends to give some appearance of legality to the military usurpers and the agents of colonial rule who have illegally seized power in some parts of the Congo.

Shortly after independence the Congolese army mutinied. Patrice Lumumba and his colleagues had to secure outside support from somewhere if they were to preserve the legal structure of the State.

In the interests of world peace and in order to prevent the cold war being brought into Africa, Patrice Lumumba invited the United Nations to preserve law and order. The United Nations insisted that they should have the sole mandate to do this and that the legal Government of the Congo should not obtain that military assistance which would have otherwise been forthcoming form many other friendly African States

However, instead of preserving law and order, the United Nations declared itself neutral between law and disorder and refused to and lend any assistance whatsoever to the legal Government in suppressing the mutineers who had set themselves up in power in Katanga and South Kasai.

When, in order to move its troops against the rebels the Government of the Congo obtained some civilian aircraft and civilian motor vehicles from the Soviet Union, the colonialist Powers at the United Nations raised a howl of rage while, at the same time, maintaining a discreet silence over the build-up of Belgian arms and actual Belgian military forces in the service of the rebels.

With a total disregard of the Constitution, which expressly provided that the President could not dismiss the Prime Minister unless there had been a vote of "no confidence" in the parliament, Kasavubu illegally tried to remove Patrice Lumumba from office and to substitute another Government. When Lumumba wishes to broadcast to the people, explaining what had happened, the United Nations in the so called interest of law and order prevented him by force from speaking.

They did not, however, use the same force to prevent the mutineers of the Congolese Army from seizing power in Leopoldville and installing a completely illegal Government.

Despite the fact that one of the most important reasons for the United Nations action was supposedly to see that all Belgian forces were removed, the United Nations sat by while the so-called Katanga Government, which is entirely Belgian-controlled, imported aircraft and arms from Belgium and from other countries, such as South Africa which have a vested interest in the suppression of African freedom. The United Nations connived at the setting up, in fact, of an independent Katanga State, though this is contrary to the Security Council's own resolutions.

Finally, the United Nations, which could exert its authority to prevent Patrice Lumumba from broadcasting, was, so it pleaded, quite unable to prevent his arrest by mutineers or his transfer, through the use of airfields under United Nations control, into the hands of the Belgian-dominated Government of Katanga.

The United Nations is, on behalf of all its members, in control of the finances of the Congo. It is now two months ago since I personally wrote to Mr. Hammerskjoeld to ask him where the money came from which is being used to pay the soldiers in Mobutu's illegal army. I am still awaiting for an answer. One thing is certain, however, this money does not come from the revenue of the Congo. It is supplied from outside by those who wish to restore colonialism in practice by maintaining in office a puppet regime entirely financially dependent upon them.

The time has come to speak plainly. The danger in the Congo is not so mush the possibility of a civil war between Africans, but rather a colonialist war in which the colonial and imperialist powers hide behind African puppet regimes.

At this very moment Northern Katanga is being laid waste by military units under command of a regular officer of the Belgian army, Colonel Crevecoeur, armed with the most modern weapons, supplied by Belgium.

Recruiting offices have been opened in South Africa, in France, and elsewhere, and wages of over four hundred pounds a month are being offered to former German fascist officers and to former collaborators of Hitler and Mussolini in other countries in order to persuade them to enlist in an unholy war against the African people.

Where, I ask again, does the money come from to pay these big salaries and to buy all of this modern and expensive armament which is now being deployed against unarmed peasants and villagers?

The rulers of the United States, of the United Kingdom, of France and of the other powers who are militarily allied with Belgium, must answer these questions

Why did they express so loudly their indignation when the Soviet Union placed at the disposal of the legal Government of the Congo civilian aircraft and civilian vehicles? Why are they so silent when their ally, Belgium, openly supplies military aircraft and armoured vehicles to the rebel? Why is it that no single member of the North Atlantic Treaty Organisation has on any occasion addressed to Belgium any public rebuke for the flagrant breaches of the Security Council resolution in which Belgium is every day indulging? Alas, the architects of this murder are many.

In Ghana we realise the great financial stakes which some great powers have in the United Miniere and in other industrial and commercial undertakings in the Congo. I would, however, ask these powers these questions: Do they really believe that ultimately they can safeguard they their investments and their interests in the Congo by convening at a brutal and savage colonialist war?

Do they realised that they are sacrificing African lives to continue in Africa the cold war at the very time when all powers, both great and small, should be concentrating on the abolition of colonialism and establishment of world peace?

Patrice Lumumba, Maurice Mpolo and Joseph Okito have died because they put their faith in the United Nations and because they refused to allow themselves to be used as stooges or puppets for external interests.

There is still time for those who have supported this cruel colonialist war in the Congo to change their policy, but time is running out.

The cynical planning of the murder of Patrice Lumumba and his colleagues as is a final lesson for us all. We cannot ignore the fact that this crime show every evidence of the most careful preparation and timing. First there came the handing over of Patrice Lumumba and others to the Belgian-controlled authorities in Katanga.

Next there came the contemptuous refusal of these same authorities to allow the United Nations Conciliation Committee any access to the prisoners. From this came the final proof that the United Nations would not effectively intervene to save the lives of the Prime Minister or his colleagues. This was followed by the formation of the so-called new Kasavubu Government and the warning by Belgium to Belgian nationals to leave those parts of the Congo controlled by the legal Government.

Finally came the story so reminiscent of Nazi and Fascist technique—the false account of an attempt to escape and the death of the prisoners following upon it.

What are the next steps in this plan? The information before me now is that the Kasavubu-Mobutu group has planned an offensive against Orientale Province in an attempt to secure a quick military victory before the Security Council can deal with the matter.

My information is that this plan has been made with the full knowledge of the French and Belgian Governments and has their full support.

Let me issue a most serious warning: Any such action, unless immediately denounced by the other members of the Security Council, will have a profound effect on African relations with the great powers.

Our dear brothers, Patrice Lumumba, Maurice Mpolo and Joseph Okito are dead, and I ask you all to join with me in mourning the loss which the whole African continent has sustained through their cruel murder. But their spirit is not dead, nor are the things for which they stood: African freedom, the unity and independence of Africa, and the final and complete destruction of colonialism and imperialism.

The colonialists and imperialists have killed them but what they cannot do, is to kill the ideals which we still preach, and for which they sacrificed their lives.

In the Africa of the future their names will live for ever more.

A Message of Condolence sent by the Osagyefo on February 14, 1961, to Madam Lumumba on the death of her husband

The cruel murder of your beloved husband and our dear brother and comrade in the struggle for liberation of the African continent, has come not only as a personal shock to me but also as a tragedy which the Government and people of Ghana and the rest of the African continent cannot easily forget.

The Government and people of Ghana join me in sending you our deepest condolence for a loss which does not only rob you and your children of a dear husband and father but deprives the whole of Africa of the counsel of one of its noblest sons of our age.

I loved Patrice both as a person and as a politician with both a vision and a message for Africa and you and I, as well as all patriotic sons of Africa, shall miss him dearly.

In this terrible hour, I urge you to be consoled by the fact that your dear husband died in a just and noble cause; his memory shall not be dulled by passage of years nor shall time extinguish the flame he has kindled in the hearts of many; Africa shall always remember him as one of its greatest sons, who laid down his life that Africa might be free.

May God bless his soul.

An official statement issued by the office of the President on the situation in the Congo following the death of Mr. Lumumba.

The Government of Ghana has noted with considerable concern a press statement attributed to the President of the United States and to the effect that the only legal authority entitled to speak for the Congo as a whole is a Government established under the Chief of State, President Kasavubu.

Under the Constitution of the Congolese Republic, President Kasavubu has no executive powers and is a constitutional ruler in the same sense as is the King of the Belgians.

The Constitution of the Congo was unanimously agreed upon by all political parties, including that of Mr. Kasavubu and of Mr. Tshombe at the round table conference in Brussels. Under this Constitution the powers of the President are purely ceremonial, as are those of the King of the Belgians. In particular, the President is not entitled to dismiss a Government unless there is a vote of no confidence in both Houses of Parliament carried by an absolute majority of the Members of each House. Alternatively, the Government may be dismissed if there is a vote of no confidence carried by two-thirds of the Members present and voting in the Chambers sitting together. Before a new Government can be legally installed it must receive a lot of confidence in both Houses of Parliament and until the new Government has received this vote of confidence the outgoing Government remains in office.

The alleged appointment by President Kasavubu of a new Government in place of that of the late Mr. Lumumba was thus doubly illegal. In the first place there was no vote of no confidence in Mr. Lumumba's Government, without which the President was not entitled in law to dismiss the Government and secondly, the Government which he subsequently claimed to install never received a vote of confidence from Parliament. Even, therefore, if President Kasavubu had been entitled to dismiss Mr. Lumumba's Government, which he was not, under the Constitution Mr. Lumumba's Government remained in power until a new Government obtained a vote of confidence in Parliament. There can thus be no doubt that under the Constitution of the Congo the only legal and legitimate Government is that formed by the late Mr. Lumumba and now established under Mr. Gizenga in Stanleyville.

Under the principles of international law it is improper to recognise a revolutionary Government which is based upon the overthrow of the Constitution unless it is at least in de facto control of the country.

In fact, the so-called Government which have been set up by Mr. Kasavubu have been in control of nothing. All effective power in Leopoldville has been in the hands of a mutinous soldier, Colonel Mobutu, who claimed that he had deposed Mr. Kasavubu and who forcibly prevented Parliament from meeting.

In the view of the Government of Ghana the statement attributed by the press to President Kennedy marks a most dangerous departure from the principles of international law and is likely considerably to aggravate the situation in the Congo.

It is quite true that from time to time countries with a democratic form of Government have acknowledged regimes which have arisen through the overthrow by force of the Constitution of the country concerned and which have involved the suppression of all parliamentary institutions. There is however, a fundamental difference between the case of the Congo and that of other suppressions of democratic regimes by force. In the case of the Congo, the United Nations were invited to send their armed forces to the Republic by the legitimate Government which had been installed in office strictly in accordance with the Constitution.

During the period when the United Nations were in occupation, this legitimate Government was overthrown by a military revolt and an entirely unconstitutional regime established. The Government of Ghana takes the most serious view of the fact that apparently one permanent member of the Security Council is prepared to acknowledge the legitimacy of a Government formed in such circumstances. If such a principle were to be generally accepted it would destroy the whole basis upon which United Nations aid has hitherto been granted to legitimate Governments seeking support against external aggression. The very fact that United Nations troops are in any particular country means that that country must forego the aid which it would normally receive from other friendly states to preserve its internal security. The presence of United Nations forces in control of airfields and of the means of communications limits the powers of the Government which has invited these forces into its country and makes it very difficult for that Government to deal with subversion from within. If now the principle is to be accepted that if under such circumstances a revolt can be engineered permanent members of the Security Council are entitled to acknowledge as legitimate a military dictatorship based on the suppression of all parliamentary liberties and institutions, then democracy is everywhere endangered.

It would appear from the press reports of President Kennedy's statement that the President of the United States justified his action by stating that President Kasavubu has been seated in the General Assembly of the United Nations by a majority vote of its members. If President Kennedy has been correctly reported, this would appear to be a complete misunderstanding of the principles of international law as they are understood by the Government of Ghana. All Heads of State are seated in the United Nations in the sense that they personify the country of which they are the head. In the case of a constitutional Monarch or President, however, this is a purely theoretical conception. The Queen of the United Kingdom, for example, is also seated in the United Nations as the Queen of Canada, Australia, New Zealand, South Africa, and Ceylon and has, indeed, addressed the United Nations in this joint capacity. The constitutional Government theory apparently advanced by President Kennedy to justify the United States recognition of the unconstitutional Government of the Congo is that the Queen in her personal capacity would be entitled to dismiss say, the Government of Canada or Ceylon and that the United Nations would be bound to seat whatever Government she might nominate in their place, irrespective of the provisions of the Constitutions of Canada or Ceylon.

The Government of Ghana has invited the Ambassador of the United States in Ghana to seek clarification of the statesment made by President Kennedy since the Government of Ghana is most reluctant to believe that he would have put forward a constitutional proposition of this nature.

It is quite true that the United Nations did seat a delegation which had been nominated by President Kasavubu, but which had not been endorsed by the legitimate Government of the Republic of the Congo. At this time, however, Mobutu was commanding some of the Congolese troops in Leopoldville and announced that by the end of the year he was proposing to relinquish the authority which he had seized by force and to permit Parliament to re-assemble. The vote in favour of seating the delegation nominated by President Kasabuvu was in a large degree secured by the belief among some countries that constitutional Government was about to be restored and that either the Government nominated by President Kasavubu would receive parliamentary approval, or else another Government, which has the support of Parliament, would be formed.

It is, however, most important to note that the proposal to seat this delegation was not supported by any one whatsoever of the countries which had supplied continents of troops for service in the Congo. No single country represented on the Conciliation Committee voted in favour of this proposal, which was considered by the countries which had experience of Congo conditions as most unlikely to lead to any good result.

The Government of Ghana therefore, much regrets that the Government of the United States should justify its action in acknowledging a Government based on the suppression of all parliamentary institutions and liberties by a vote in the United Nations which all those countries concerned most intimately with the affairs of the Congo were unanimously unable to support.

Extract from an address made by Osagyefo Dr. Kwame Nkrumah, President of the Republic of Ghana, at the laying of the foundation stone of the Kwame Nkrumah Institute, Winneba

on February 18, 1961.

Comrades and Friends:

At this very moment, Ghana mourns the death by brutal murder of Patrice Lumumba, late Prime Minister of the Congo, and his two associates Mpolo and Okito.

We at this gathering should do honour to their memory. But before I call for the observance of a two-minute silence, I wish to say this: Up to today the murders of Premier Lumumba and his two associates Mpolo and Okito, have been clouded in mystery.

The childish story of villagers killing these stalwart freedom fighters is the most absurd fabrication, that could emanate only from the diseased brains of Belgian colonialists and their puppet agents.

But just this very afternoon, it has been revealed to me by a reliable source that the murder of Patrice Lumumba, of Maurice

Mpolo and of Joseph Okito took place on January 18th.

The information reveals that the men were sent for, one by one, and commanded to kneel and pray. Then, as he prayed, each was shot in the back by the order of a Belgian officer.

When Patrice Lumumba knelt to pray, the African soldier who was ordered to shoot him refused to do so whereupon the Belgian officer took his revolver and shot Lumumba himself.

I have narrated these facts, not in any desire further to hurt your already wounded hearts. On the contrary, I have done so in order that you who pass through this institute, which I am proud to say bears my name, and which will stand forever for the principles and ideals for which I have always stood and eternally stand, may know the diabolical depths of degradation to which these twin-monsters of imperialism and colonialism can descend. You will then be able to assess the magnitude of the task still ahead and offer yourselves in unity.

Let us all stand up in silence for two minutes for our murdered brothers and comrades in arms.

And now, comrades and friends, it is my most pleasant duty to declare the foundation stone of the Kwame Nkrumah Institute well and truly laid. I feel happy to declare also the first course of the Ideological Training Centre of the institute duly inaugurated.

Thank you.

A Message from Osagyefo Dr. Kwame Nkrumah, President of the Republic of Ghana, to the Secretary General of the United Nations.
February 20, 1961.

It is now time that a new and serious approach be made to the present ineffective efforts of the United Nations in the Congo if the United Nations is to be saved and the future peace of Africa assured.

As I indicated at the beginning of the operations in the Congo, the problem must be tackled in two phases— first, the military problem and second the political one. Unless the military problem can be solved first there can be no lasting political solution.

I would like to come to New York to give my views on both phases because I am certain that from now on the initiative must come from the African countries with military support from the Asian bloc. All initiative and aid from the big or NATO powers should cease. The flow of arms and equipment into the Congo provides conditions which could lead to a civil war of the Spanish type, with grave consequences throughout the whole world.

All Belgian military, paramilitary and other personnel serving the various factions should be expelled from the Congo at once. All non-African and Asian military personnel not specifically require to work under the United Nations Command must leave the Congo.

The situation is so serious that in my view the interpretation of the Security Council Mandate, namely, non-interference in the internal affairs of the Congo, is no longer tenable. The plan which I envisage for dealing with the present situation is as follows:-

(a) A new United Nations Command should be established in the Congo;

(b) This Command must be African and should take over complete responsibility for law and order in the Congo.

(c) All Congolese armed units should be disarmed; this disarming will involve their return to barracks and the surrender of their weapons to the new United Nations Command;

(d) The disarming and hand-over should be voluntary, and should lead to the re-organisation and re-training of the Congolese National Army; but if certain factions will not co-operate, force must be used;

(e) All non-African personnel serving in the Congolese Army must be expelled immediately.

(f) Once the military situation has been brought under control on these lines, all political prisoners must be released by the new United Nations Command, and the new Command should then convene Parliament under its auspices.

(g) All foreign Diplomatic Missions and representatives should immediately leave the Congo for the time being,

in order to give this new United Nations Command a fair chance and to eliminate the cold war from the Congo.

In view of the importance of this matter, I propose that you should circulate this communication to members of the Security Council and I am releasing the contents of this telegram to the press at 1800 Hours GMT.

Awaiting your reply earliest.

4

THE VOLTA RIVER PROJECT

NATIONAL ASSEMBLY

Accra
February 21, 1961

MR. SPEAKER, MEMBERS OF THE NATIONAL ASSEMBLY,

I have stated on a number of occasions in the past that Parliament would, at the appropriate time, be given an opportunity to discuss the Volta River Project. That appropriate time is today, when I wish to inform Members of the National Assembly of the position now reached in regard to the Volta River Project, and to give them the long-promised opportunity to hear of the various actions taken by the Government on this all-important project. A debate will be taken on a substantive motion after my statement, and I hope the House will at the conclusion of that debate, endorse action so far taken by the Government, and authorise the final negotiations to proceed in order that the project may start this year.

I have made no secret of the fact, and I remain firmly convinced that Ghana must progress towards a balanced economy and this means the creation, where nothing existed before, of an industrial sector of our economy which can balance the agricultural potentialities which we are already developing. Members are aware that a number of steps in this direction have already been taken with the creation, either by the Government or, with the encouragement of the Government by private enterprise, of a number of industries of varying size and importance.

Recently the Government has made an offer to the shareholders of five gold mines. This offer, if accepted, will mean that the State will own mines which last year produced 58 per cent of Ghana's total output of gold. If, therefore, the offer is accepted, the State will own an important share in one of the leading heavy industries of the country.

But I have always felt that it is necessary to provide, in a far more effective manner than hitherto, the means whereby industrialisation can be accelerated. All industries of any major economic significance require, as a basic facility, a large and reliable source of power. In fact, the industrialisation of Europe, of America, of Canada, of Russia and of other countries, emerged as a result of the invention of sources of power of hitherto undreamt of size. Newer nations, such as ours, which are determined by every possible means to catch up in industrial strength, must have elect any large-scale industrial advance. Electricity is the basis for industrialisation.

That, basically, is the justification for the Volta River Project. There are other very sound reasons which I will mention in a moment but, first, I will like to sketch in brief the events which have made it possible, for the first time, for a definite proposal before this House.

As is stated in the White Paper now on the Table of the House, my Party was first to promise in an election manifesto in 1951, that when voted to power, it would do everything possible to harness power from the Volta. As a result of this determination, my Government pursued the project through various stages, culminating in the Preparatory Commission whose report was published in 1956. We had all hoped at that time that we would be able to proceed with the scheme as it was then planned, and much work and considerable sums of money were spent in arranging for exhibitions and descriptions of the scheme to be sent to all parts of the country so that the people would know what was proposed and why.

Unfortunately, the timing, in terms of international financing, coincided with financial stringency when interest rates on loans and lengths of loans repayments became less favourable and world demand for aluminium was temporarily outstripped by production capacity. We therefore found it was not at that time advisable to go ahead with a scheme which might have cost, in total, as much as three hundred million pounds. This original scheme was extremely comprehensive and covered the complete operation of producing aluminium metal from raw bauxite, including the building of the towns, the railways, the roads and a special harbour, by the Government, and a mine, alumina plant, and smelter by the aluminium companies. Since then protracted discussions and negotiations have been continuing with a view to improving the scheme to make it more attractive financially. The Government had already in 1953 decided that a new harbour at Tema and a new township there would be necessary in any case, regardless of whether the Volta scheme went ahead or not, and this has much reduced the costs attributable to the project. The world financing position has tended recently to be more stable so that it is possible to plan with rather more assurance that situations will not alter so rapidly as to render a scheme, which is possible this year, hopelessly uneconomic next year.

During the period since 1956, I have been at pains to explore every possible way of bringing this scheme to life. I have sought the assistance of friendly Governments and, in particular, the Government of the United States of America, with whose President I raised in October 1957 the desirability of pressing forward the scheme. President Eisenhower was sympathetic to my aspirations, and arranged for the International Co-operation Administration to assist in finding ways and means of making the project attractive. Arising out of the advice of this body, it was decided that the project should be re-appraised to examine the engineers aspects of developing the power of the Volta waters and to make an appreciation of the economics of the project. The Henry J. Kaiser Company, a leading American firm of engineers, was selected to undertake this re-appraisal and, in February, 1959, submitted to the Government "The Reassessment Report on the Volta River Project."

By now it had became clear that the original basis of a type of financial partnership between the Government and aluminium producers would not be the best way to tackle the problem and our Government decided that the power development should be undertaken from public resources, while the development of a smelter should be a matter for private enterprise purchasing power on a purely commercial basis; it was also considered that it would be better to defer the production of alumina from Ghana bauxite, so that the cost of the smelter can use imported alumina, in order to reduce the heavy initial capital cost of the project.

It is desirable to mention briefly why it is necessary for an aluminium smelter to be encouraged to establish itself and to purchase power from the Volta project. The project involves damming a very large river; the flow of the Volta River varies in the ratio of as much as 300 to 1 between flood and low water, and, therefore, to obtain the maximum power from the Volta means creating a large lake which will provide a reserve of water for the low water season and will without danger absorb the large quantities of water which flow during the floods. To build a small dam and power house would be very uneconomic and would lead to considerable waste of water, because the lake area would be too small to absorb all the flood.

The proposed dam will provide a steady flow of water sufficient to generate from Akosombo alone electricity more than twenty times greater than the total installed capacity of the Electricity Department in 2960. If electricity is to be sold economically, the price will have to be calculated by dividing the annual outgoings of the project, which include loan servicing, by the number of units of electricity actually sold. Therefore, the Volta project would be uneconomical if it sold electricity only to the Electricity Department and did not have another major customer to reduce the initial cost of the power by sharing the bill. A smelter, which produces metal by passing a very heavy current of electricity through alumina powder, is the only major industry which consumes a very large and steady current of electricity. By encouraging a smelter to establish itself in Ghana, the Government becomes assured of a steady sale of electricity, in our case approximately 300,000 kilowatts. This immediately reduces the overall cost of generating electricity so that the balance can be sold to the Electricity Department at a reasonable and economic figure.

The Reassessment Report recommended the construction of the dam at Akosombo rather than Ajena and, when all the power produced from this development was committed, the extension of the scheme by the provision of a smelter power station at Kpong would provide an additional 86,000 kilowatts of power. The Report also recommended, as a further development, if necessary, the establishment of hydro-electric station at Bui, and Members will recollect that the Government has recently reached agreement with the Soviet Union for the design and construction of this station.

The original Volta River Project was designed to provide the bulk of the electricity produced by the dam to an aluminium smelter, and a comparatively small proportion only would have been made available for domestic consumption in Ghana. The Kaiser Reassessment Report, on the other hand, recommended the installation of a national electricity grid system covering the major part of southern Ghana from Tema through Accra, Cape Coast, Takoradi, Tarkwa, Dunkwa, Kumasi, Koforidua and back to Akosombo. At selected points on the national grid would be provided outlets from which the Electricity Department would distribute electricity for domestic and industrial users in a wide area, and the routing of the grid would also provide outlets for power supplies to many of the larger mines.

In fact, the amount of electricity would be sufficient, if transmission lines could be installed economically, to provide power for the whole country, and even to sell some power to our sister neighbouring countries. This scheme was accepted in principle by the Government, not only because it provided for reasonable economic operation of the scheme in the early years by selling power to a smelter but also because it would provide a large and reliable source of electric power for many years to come for Ghana's development.

As I already mentioned, I have arranged for the details of the project to be set out in a White Paper which has been placed on the Table of the House this morning. This Paper contains the details of the scheme, and I commend it to Members for their study and approval. It will be seen from this Paper that the project provides for a return on the money invested in such a way that, in addition to the scheme being fully self-liquidation over the period of its estimated life of fifty years, the financial returns should suffice to cover from its own earnings any future power development which may be required by Ghana. The cost of the scheme is estimated to be just over G£70$\frac{1}{2}$ million for the public utility sector consisting of the dam, power house, transmission lines and substations, including provision for the resettlement of the people whose area will be flooded by the lake which the dam will create. This will cover 3,275 square miles and will be the largest man-made lake in the world. Also included is the cost of establishing a Volta River Authority which will be charged with the task of constructing and operating the project, and the cost of health measures to ensure the prevention of epidemics which might arise as a result of the creation of the lake.

Seventy and a half Million Pounds (Ghana) is a lot of money.

To implement the project will mean a real sacrifice for the people of Ghana, and in order that everyone may be fully aware of the reasons why I consider this scheme to be worthwhile, I wish to mention briefly some of the advantages which will accrue from it.

In the first place, the provision of the power and transmission system will remove one of the obstacles in the way of our rapid industrialisation, because, once the scheme is built power will be available for sale to any industry, moreover, it is well known that industrial development follows the provision of adequate and reliable supplies of power—power to drive machinery, power to process materials, power to provide refrigeration, power to operate chemical processes and, of course, power to smelt aluminum and other materials.

Secondly, the smelter itself will at one stroke provide a new major industry for Ghana. I am aware that in certain quarters there is doubt regarding the sincerity of the Government's wish to encourage, as part of the overall development of Ghana, the private sector of the economy. The establishment of a smelter will cost its owners in the region of £100 million. For so large an investment special arrangements are necessary and this House will be asked specifically to approve the terms of the agreement which is to be entered into between the Government and the Volta Aluminum Company Limited to be commonly known as VALCO. It will, however, be noted that the Government's agreement with VALCO provides for certain simple changes in our legislation, which have already been approved by this House, and that the general provisions of our law are such that a private company is sufficiently encouraged to undertake so very great an investment. When it is remembered that this private company has been formed by some of the world's greatest producers of aluminium, this willingness to invest in Ghana's future at once gives the lie to those who wish to cast doubts on our intentions.

The smelter will employ about 1,500 persons when in operation; once its pioneer company relief period is over, it will be paying company taxes to he Ghana Government; and the company will pay to the Volta River Authority nearly £2$\frac{1}{2}$ million per year for electricity.

The third advantage to be derived from the project will be the increase in Ghana's foreign exchange which will accrue from the operations of the smelter. We will, in effect, be exporting electricity and we will be exporting the work of the smelter's employees. Let me explain how this comes about. The smelter will be bringing to Ghana, in the early stages, the alumina powder for conversion into aluminum metal. This process, as I have already mentioned, involves passing large quantities of electricity through the powder, thereby melting out the metal. When the aluminium ingot emerges at the end of the process, electricity has, in effect been incorporated in it and the cost of electricity will have been paid for, in the processing charge, by VALCO's foreign purchasers of the metal. Into the production of the aluminium will also have gone the work of the smelter's employees, and this will have been paid for, in the processing charge, by VALCO's foreign customers. And so Ghana's work and Ghana's electricity will have gone abroad to earn foreign exchange for our country.

Fourthly, the creation of a lake such that which the scheme envisages will provide a new highway from the dam up to the Northern Region. The Government has arranged for a survey to be conducted by Kaiser Engineers to report to me on the prospects of containing that water highway to the sea, so that ships may transport bulk materials to the Northern Region, and may bring back the cattle and produce of the north to southern Ghana, thereby developing inland trade by providing cheap transportation. Moreover, in northeast Ghana near the head of that branch of the lake which will cover what is now the Oti River, there are deposits of iron ore which will, we hope, be exploited to provide the raw material for a ferro-manganese plant and iron smelter. Plans for this are also being worked out, as part of our industrialisation programme.

A fifth advantage which will accrue to Ghana from this project is the creation of a very large source of fish, The lake will, it is estimated, eventually produce up to 10,000 tons of fresh fish a year, much of it readily accessible to areas of Ghana too far from the sea for our sea-water catches to be readily transported there. The lake fishing industry can became important, and it is proposed to develop this as soon as the lake has filed and the fish have had time to multiply.

A further advantage is that about six hundred square miles of land around the shores of the lake will be flooded each season at high water, and should prove amenable to intensive cultivation of crops such as rice, and it is the intention of the Government to increase Ghana's food production by making the best possible use of this land.

Although, therefore, this scheme is costly, it is my view and the view of the Government that the advantages which will accrue from it very fully justify us in taking every possible step to bring it to fruition.

I wish to discuss briefly the method by which the money which we need for the scheme is to be found. The Government has completed preliminary discussions with the International Bank for Reconstruction and Development, the Development Loan Fund of the United States, the United Kingdom Government and the Export-Import Bank of Washington, for loans amounting to a total of thirty million pounds, I approached the previous President of the United States of America with regard to the provision of an additional loan of approximately ten million pounds to provide for the national transmission system, and it hoped to make arrangements for this money also. Finally, it is proposed to provide up to a maximum of thirty-five million pounds from our own development fund as an equity investment in the scheme. While the details of the loan agreements between the Government and the organisations I have mentioned are not yet final, it is expected that these will be finalised in the course of the next two or three months, thus ensuring that when the tender is awarded, the financial arrangements will all have been completed.

The Reassessment Report on the Volta River Project was received in February, 1959. Whenever any large project of this nature is undertaken, a great deal of time can be wasted in initial preparatory work on the site, including such matters as the provision of access roads, housing for the construction staff, and water and power facilities during the construction phase. I have been confident throughout that we would succeed in bringing the Volta scheme to life and the Government has accordingly undertaken, by arrangement with the Kaiser group, for the bulk of this preparatory work to be completed in advance of the letting of the contract for the dam and power house, so that, when the contractor arrives to start work, he will find a site ready for his occupation. Our faith in this scheme is now visible at Akosombo in the shape of houses, a power station, water supplies and a first class access road. We have, in fact, already created the nucleus of a modern township and are continuing the preliminary works, which can be used by the contractor during the construction of the project and which can afterwards develop into the township serving as lake port at Akosombo and accommodating the staff operating the project itself. Arrangements have been made for the preliminary works to be integrated into an overall town plan which will cover Akosombo's future growth and development, and Doxiades Associates have been engaged to undertake this work. One of the criteria which has been adopted is that of keeping the site of the dam and power station free from ugly and depressing buildings, so that the area can be made into a true attraction for tourists, not only because of the world-wide interest which so great a project will arouse, bust also because the area will be made into a delight to the eye.

I have in mind a plan whereby, without any loss of power water can be diverted from the dam so as to provide a series of fountains and pools set in terraced gardens which climb up to a first-class hotel. At night the fountains can be lit by thousands of multi-coloured lights.

I have already mentioned the amount of power which the Volta River Project is designed to produce and wish now to give a few details of the project itself to give Members an idea of the vast size of this work. The main dam across the river will be 2,100 feet, or 700 yards, long at its crest. It will in effect be a large hill built of rock with waterproof clay core in the centre, It will be 370 feet high, and will require a total 10.9 million cubic yards of rock and clay. By comparison, it will be four-and a half times longer and nearly five times higher than the Ambassador Hotel building. Looking up-river, there is a valley to the right of the dam which will also have to be closed by a smaller dam 1,200 feet long and 120 feet high and, between the two dams, will be a spillway structure to control flood water. On the left, looking up stream, will be the intake structure level with the top of the dam, and the power house some 200 feet below. Between the two will be six penstocks which are 24-foot diameter pipes, to feed the water from the intake structure into the turbines driving the electricity generators. Thus, each penstock would be big enough to take two double decked buses side by side, and still leave plenty of room. The power house will be designed to take six generators, each of 128,000 kilowatts continuous output, and each will be designed for 15 per cent overload. The rotating part of each generator will be about 35 feet in diameter and will weigh nearly 500 tons. The power house will be about 560 feet long, 130 feet high, and 170 feet deep. In order to transform the voltage produced by the generators to the 161,000 volts of the transmission net, each generator will have a transformer which will weigh nearly 150 tons and will be 20 feet high by 16 feet wide, The transmission system will be about 270 miles long. When completed, it will be fair to say that this dam and power station will be one of the major engineering feats of the world.

The work of constructing this enormous project has been divided into a main engineering contract, tenders for which have recently been received, which will cover the construction of the dams, the power house and the spillway structures and other contracts providing for the supply of the electrical, mechanical and transmission equipment, together with the sub-stations. During the peak of the construction phase, it is estimated that over 3,000 workers will be required on the dams and power station, consisting of over 20 specialised traders. The task of assembling so impressive a force of construction workers without seriously disrupting other development work in Ghana, is itself a matter for very careful planning, and arrangements are being made for lists of potential workers to be held ready and for initial training schemes to be conducted in those skills which are not at present available in Ghana. It is planned that the contract should be let in April this year and that the work should be completed, and first power should start flowing down the transmission cables, in September, 1965.

As I have already mentioned, the success of this project depends on the purchase of electricity. We have arranged on the one hand for as large block of electricity to be sold to an aluminum smelter. The only other direct purchase of electricity from the Volta River Authority is to be the Electricity Division of the Ministry of

Works and Housing—probably in a more commercial form than at present. Clearly, therefore, the greater the amount of electricity which the Electricity Division can purchase, the more economically favourable the whole project will become. This fact has long been appreciated and not only is the Electricity Division taking steps to extend, reconstruct and reinforce its present distribution systems at those centres to be supplied from the proposed Volta grid, but on account of the present shortage of engineering staff in that Division, consideration is also being given now to the appointment of a consultant to assist the Division in the planning and design of future extensions at these centres. The aim of this two-way effort is to ensure that when power becomes available from the Volta, there should be no restriction whatsoever on the amount of electricity that any centre can take, due to any inadequacy of the distribution network at that centre. A contract has already been let for the construction of two transmission lines from Tema to Accra which will initially serve to convey power from the new Tema diesel power station to Accra, and eventually be incorporated in the national grid. This work is expected to be completed by September of this year.

In considering electricity consumption in Ghana, the potentialities of the various mines in the country has not been overlooked. It is a fact that the amount of electricity generated by these mines, for their own requirements, is some 50 per cent more than the total electricity generated by the stations of the Electricity Division at present. In order to further enhance the economic viability of the national grid system, therefore, it has been planned to supply as many of these mines as the costs of the particular sections or extensions of the transmission line prove economically justifiable.

I have mentioned already that special arrangements have been entered into to encourage an aluminium smelter to establish itself in Ghana, and I shall now describe in general terms what these arrangements are. The Volta Aluminium Company Limited was formed towards the end of 1959 by a consortium of aluminium manufacturers under the leadership of the Kaiser Aluminium and Chemical Corporation. It included Reynolds Metals, the Aluminium Company of America, and Olin Mathieson. On the 16th December, 1959, I signed, on behalf of the Government of Ghana, a statement of the principles upon which it would be feasible to establish a smelter, and the principles of Agreement were signed on behalf of VALCO, as the Volta Aluminium Company is now known, by Mr. Rhoades, the President of the Kaiser Aluminium and Chemical Corporation. These Principles of Agreement formed the starting point for detailed negotiations with VALCO which were conducted during 1960, and which ended on the 17th of November, 1960, with the informal signing of a complex of documents, known as the Master agreement and its scheduled documents by the Minister of Finance on behalf of the Government and by Mr. Edgar Kaiser on behalf of VALCO.

I would like at this point to pay a tribute, and a very well deserved tribute, to Mr. Edgar Kaiser and his associates, including Mr. Chad Calhoun. Ever since his organisation was brought into the Volta River Project to conduct an engineering re-appraisal, Mr. Edgar Kaiser has demonstrated enthusiasm and understanding of the project, and of the problems which have faced us in bringing it to life, which is second only to our own. He and his associates have helped with the engineering design and have been instrumental in bringing the concept of an aluminium smelter in Ghana forward to the stage of practical realisation.

The Master Agreement between Ghana and VALCO is designed to provide the conditions under which the smelter and later, the alumina plant and bauxite mines would operate. It includes provision for VALCO to provide the necessary finance and to construct a smelter, the rate of expansion of the smelter to its initial planned capacity of about 135,000 long tons of ingot per annum, consuming 300,000 kilowatts power continuously; and the establishment of special trust arrangement for these funds to ensure that VALCO's obligations are met. It provides for investment in the power project by the Government; for the establishment by the Government of a Volta River Authority for special arrangements for charges for processing alumina, for payment for water, port facilities and communications; for the employment and training of Ghanaians to the greatest feasible extent; for arrangements for the application of the new pioneer relief legislation to VALCO for tax stabilisation and for exchange control measures in regard to VALCO's earnings in foreign currency and for the execution of associated contracts. Of these, the most important is the power contract which provides for the long-term purchase of, and the charges for a block of the power to be produced at Akosombo. This power contract is to be executed by the Volta River Authority when it is established, and it is the intention to introduce, during the current meeting of the Assembly, a Bill to set up the Volta River Authority as a statutory corporation. The purchase of power is provided for in Article 13 of the power contract and the effect of this article in terms of revenue to the project is set out in Chapter 5 paragraph 9, of of the White Paper; this chapter also explains the reasons for the application to VALCO of a special contract price for the sale of power.

Other documents which will have to be executed are the smelter Site Lease, the Water Agreement and the Port Agreement, the terms of which are self-explanatory and are set out in the White Paper. It will be noted that the Master Agreement provides for a series of transactions which must be satisfactorily concluded before the agreements can come into effect. These "trigger" arrangements are set out in Article 47 of the Master Agreement, and it will be noted that the first of these is signification by this Assembly of approval of a formal resolution endorsing the Government's action and the conditions of the Agreements. They include also the satisfactory conclusion of arrangements for financing the power project and the finalisation, on terms satisfactory to the Government, of a number of special financial and trust arrangements to be undertaken by VALCO's shareholders. They also include the satisfactory conclusion of a tax treaty, providing for double taxation relief, between Ghana and the United States Government.

Action on all these points is continuing, and one of the purposes of the debate in this Assembly, which follows, is to seek the approval of this Assembly of the arrangement which was made and the advice of the Assembly that I should on behalf of Ghana, execute these agreements with VALCO. It has always been the intention of the Government to give the representatives of the people of Ghana a full opportunity to consider the Volta scheme in all its aspects before the Government enters into any final commitment and I hope that Members will take this opportunity of apprising themselves fully of all that is implied in this project, so that they may in turn explain its benefits to their constituents, and so that the whole of the Republic of Ghana may give to the Government and myself every support and encouragement.

To summarise, the present position is that, subject to the satisfactory conclusion of the various actions which I have described, to the satisfactory finalisation of the terms of loans from the World Bank, the United States governmental agencies, and the United Kingdom Government, and VALCO's own financing, we are ready to go ahead with the project which will, I am convinced, transform not only the geography of Ghana, but also its economy and the rate of its progress towards a balanced future.

Some of our objectives of economic and social reconstruction are high productivity and a higher standard of living for our people. I am longing for the day, and it should not be far distant, when I shall be able to abolish personal income tax in Ghana and increase wages with an effective purchasing power. But this means hard work. If we can all produce more and reduce cost, if all of us will co-operate to revolutionise our agriculture and build the many industries planned for our country, we can achieve this.

The basic necessities for these developments, apart from trained personnel, are abundant electricity and water supplies. As regards the training of personnel I have planned this for the country in the form of numerous scholarships tenable locally or abroad. The Volta, the Bui and other medium power station projects which are to start very soon will provide more than the necessary electricity and water supplies needed by the country.

Mr. Speaker, the debate in this House will be opened by the Minister of Finance, who will be moving the formal resolution seeking the approval of this House for the arrangements which have been made. I will close again inviting Members' attention to the terms of the White Paper and of the documents annexed to it, by restating my firm conviction that this project is likely to prove of the greatest possible benefit to the Government and people of our country, and by commending it the approval of this august House. Mr. Speaker, Members of the National Assembly, I leave you to your deliberations.

5

THE VISIT OF JOSIP BROZ-TITO

WELCOME ADDRESS TO THE PRESIDENT OF THE FEDERAL PEOPLE'S REPUBLIC OF YUGOSLAVIA

Tema Harbour
February 28, 1961

Mr. President,

On my own behalf and on behalf of the Government and the people of Ghana, I welcome you and your distinguished party to Ghana. We are honoured by your visit. We are particularly happy that Madam Broz has come with you and I am sure that the women of Ghana will give her a special welcome. We hope that you will all enjoy your stay here with us.

The relations between our two countries have been most cordial. We share common aspirations and I have no doubt that as a result of this visit, these aspirations and good relations will be strengthened to the advantage of both our countries.

Ghana has now embarked on a massive programme of economic, industrial and technological reconstruction for higher living and better cultural standards. We hope to show you something of our humble beginnings.

It is significant that we welcome you to-day at Tema Harbour. We hope that this huge project, so vital to the economy of Ghana, will soon be completed, and that it will be in full operation early next year. You will be able during your visit to see more of this new port and the new town which is associated with it.

On my own behalf and on behalf of the Government and people of Ghana, I formally extend to you and Madam Jovanka Broz a most hearty welcome.

*A Speech at a Dinner in honour of President Tito
Accra, March 1, 1961*

Mr. President, Madam Jovanka Broz, Ladies and Gentlemen:

The Government and people of Ghana have long looked forward to your visit, Mr. President, and when you arrived at Tema yesterday, I expressed to you and Madam Broz the joy and honour we all feel to have you with us. It is my great pleasure tonight on behalf of the Government and people of Ghana, to welcome you formally to Ghana. In doing so, I wish also to express the sincere hope that you, Sir, Madam Broz and all the members of your party, will find much to enjoy while you are here with us.

The welcome you received at Tema yesterday can be regarded as a real and sincere expression of the strong bonds of relationship which have been forged between Ghana and Yugoslavia.

You, Mr. President, have perhaps a greater and more realistic understanding than any other visitor to our shores so far, of what our struggle for freedom really means. During the long year of your own struggle to free your country from oppression, you have known the horrors and degradation of years of imprisonment and have suffered enough set-backs to crush the spirit of most determined freedom fighters in Africa. Because if this, you are one with us and it is with the greatest pride and with the spirit of true brotherhood that we welcome you to our country. The struggle that you have had and the courage and determination that you have exercised to overcome them, will serve as a great inspiration to us in this African continent who are still waging war against the evils of imperialism and colonialism.

We are particularly glad that you are accompanied by Madam Jovanka Broz, and I wish to say to her a special word of welcome. We are well aware of the courageous part that she played as a partisan during the dangerous and hectic days of your national struggle, a struggle against tremendous odds, and which could never have been won but for the determined and concerted efforts of the few, such as yourself, Mr. President, and your wife. We have the greatest admiration for her and are honoured to have so loyal and brave a freedom fighter here with us tonight. The Women of Ghana will, I am sure do everything in their power to make her stay useful and interesting.

I recall with pleasure our meeting in New York last year, and the valuable discussions we had together there. These discussions resulted in the creation of understanding between our two countries, and I believe that already concrete evidence of this can be seen to our mutual advantage.

The Government of Ghana has recently negotiated, with the Government of Yugoslavia, agreements for trade and economic and cultural co-operation. I should like also to take this opportunity to express the gratitude of the Ghana Government for the technical assistance so generously given recently to Ghana by the Government and people of Yugoslavia.

In these turbulent, anxious and trying times so ominously overcast by clouds of international tension and strife, visits of this kind go a long way towards increasing understanding among peoples.

In the past, international conferences had been the universally acknowledged medium for promoting peace and understanding among nations. The second half of the 20th century is increasingly witnessing a shifting of emphasis from international to the more intimate medium of personal visits.

We in Ghana are proud to regard the Federal People's Republic of Yugoslavia as a sister republic to Ghana, sharing the same ideals, the same concepts of the development of society and the same objective, namely, a state in which the welfare of the state cannot be divorced from the well-bring of the individual. We believe that the effort of the state should be for the material benefits of the people. In this regard, the Government and people of Ghana have watched with interest and admiration the bold stand which the Government of the Federal People's Republic of Yugoslavia has taken in the struggle for the liquidation of imperialism and colonialism. I recall, in particular, Your Excellency's speech at the plenary meeting of the United Nations General Assembly on the 22nd September, 1960, in which you asserted the natural and legitimate right of people still under racial and political domination to self-rule and self-determination. You pointed out, inter alia, on the occasion, that "the basic aspirations"—and I quote you—"of the new members of the United Nations are undoubtedly directed towards the consolidation of the independence they have achieved, towards a more rapid internal development, towards a status of equality in the community of nations, and towards a contribution of their own to the preservation of peace and to the stabilization of the world situation."

Mr. President, the aspirations of the people of this country, and indeed, of the whole of Africa, could not have been more clearly summarised.

We in this country realise that the people of the Federal People's Republic of Yugoslavia having, in the recent past, suffered severely at the hands of German fascism, appreciate to an acute degree the needs and yearnings of a people's striving to be free or to consolidate their own hard-won independence. The tragedy of the world situation of to-day is that the imperialists and colonialists refused to reconcile themselves to the simple fact that all people were created equal, were born equal, and have an equal right to self-determination, and have an equal right to manage their own affairs in their own God-given land and country. We know the strong aversion of the Government and people of Yugoslavia to colonial domination and to any form of suppression of inalienable human rights. The principles which your country stands for in the struggle for the liquidation of imperialism and colonialism in all its shapes and forms are also the main springs of our politics in Ghana.

In the conviction that the fate of the world should not be left to be determined by a few states, no matter how big, we in Ghana are committed to a policy of positive neutralism and non-alignment in the context of a continental government of Africa completely free from the dangers of the cold war.

Your visit, Mr. President, has come at a time when we have barely recovered from the shock of the brutal and humiliating murder of Practice Lumumba and his two associates. This tragic event has more than ever before exposed the wicked tactics and machinations of the imperialists and colonialists and their new-found weapons for maintaining their hold in Africa.

Never before in its fifteen years of existence has usefulness and effectiveness of the United Nations been so seriously threatened. The Congo situation in its challenging and intriguing complexity seems to have baffled this world organisation because of the simple fact that its mandate for the handling of the Congo problem has not been faithfully and vigorously prosecuted. It still remains our view that the legal Government constituted by the late Prime Minister, Mr. Lumumba, is the only legitimate Government of the Congo, and that the Government in Stanleyville of which Mr. Gizenga is the Head is the legal successor to that Government. The Government of Ghana has therefore recognised the Government now headed by Vice Premier Mr. Antonie Gizenga, and established in Stanleyville, as the only authority legally entitled to exercise the powers of Government throughout the Congo. It is a matter for satisfaction that a similar action has been taken by the Government of the Federal People's Republic of Yugoslavia.

Sir, it is one of the greatest tragedies of our day that the United Nations has drifted through half-hearted policies culminating in the cold-blooded murder of Patrice Lumumba, the legally constituted head of a popularly elected government. Lawlessness and vandalism backed by Belgian and colonialist subterfuge are the order of the day in the Congo at the present time because of the dismal failure of the United Nations policy in that country.

I make no apology, Mr. President, for dwelling so much on the tragic events in the Congo. We Ghanaians and, indeed, all Africans, see in the Congo situation the nascent forces of colonialism and imperialism which we must eradicate as soon as possible. Behind the facade of Belgian paternalism in which some, Kasavubu, Mobutu and Lolingi still appear to be steeped, we see the hydra-headed neo-colonialism slowly but clearly emerging; but that ugly head should be crushed. We believe that our own independence will be meaningless unless it is linked up with the total liberation of Africa, and we shall continue the struggle against these forces of neo-colonialism until every part of the African continent has became truly free and assumed its proper place among the galaxies of nations.

In this connection it is only right and proper and even necessary to call on all independent African states to stop dragging their feet on the ground in respect of the Congo and realise that they have a serious responsibility for the decisive defeat of imperialism: neo-colonialism manoeuvers and intriques in the Congo.

We must face this responsibility without fear and make it impossible for Belgium and her colonialist friends to twist the purpose of the United Nations to the service of their condemned interests and selfish ends.

All independent African states should adopt a firm and resolute attitude against any neo-colonialist advocacy at the next session of the United Nations General Assembly which is to lure them away from their line of duty to the Congo and to Africa. Any African state which fails in this stern duty will not only earn the total scorn of all our people but will surely stand condemned before the bar of history as traitors, despicable and un-African.

If the modern world is to cope successfully with the ever-increasing problem following in the wake of scientific and technological advancement and, indeed, if our own generation is to survive, it must be clearly accepted by the nations of the world, big and small, that the forces of nature are to be harnessed for the service of mankind and not for its destruction.

In this respect, we are fully appreciative, Mr. President, of the genuine interest of your country in the problem of disarmament and the principles of peaceful co-existence. The peoples of Africa are predominantly interested in peace—in fact we have a vested interest in peace, real peace, that will enable us to develop to the full our capabilities so deliberately stifled by our colonial oppressors for so long.

I have always maintained that colonialism breeds the germ of its own destruction and that quite apart from the effect of the sledgehammer death blows of dynamic African nationalism, this vicious system was bound to die an inglorious death from natural effects. Central African Federation provides a striking example of this process as a biological necessity. It is on the way to its sure death and nothing can save it, least of all settler intransigence. White settlement supremacy in Africa is no longer tenable. Colonialism is dying fast and we must hasten it on its way.

The Government and people of Ghana are pledged to the following aims:

(a) Complete and general disarmament;

(b) To keep the cold war out of Africa;

(c) No foreign bases in Africa;

(d) Complete abolition of the colonial system in all its forms; and

(e) To evolve a programme of social, economic, scientific, industrial and technological reconstruction with the development of a new society—a society in which the individual regardless of his origin and status, will be given equal opportunity to develop to the full his latent ability, in order to live a richer, happier life.

In this national task we see thrust on us the wider mission of working together to liberate and unite our continent and of ensuring that the millions of our brothers still denied the happiness of freedom are saved from colonialism with its appendages of poverty, fear, disease and illiteracy.

Mr. President, you will, during your stay in Ghana, see something of the rapid economic strides which we have made since attaining our independence. We know that if there is any way in which your Government can help us towards the realisation of our

aspirations of you will not hesitate to give such help. I am sure that as the bonds of friendship between our two countries grow, we shall derive mutual gains from our connections which will enable us together to play a more important role in the affairs of the world.

And now I would like to give you the toast of His Excellency the President and Madam Broz.

6

ON DEPARTURE FROM COMMONWEALTH LEADERS CONFERENCE

London
March 22, 1961

The Conference of Commonwealth Prime Ministers which has just concluded has been a most significant one. For the first time it has been necessary to examine the very foundations on which the Commonwealth rests.

I personally have refrained from commenting on the decision of South Africa to withdraw from the Commonwealth. All along it has been my view that we should do everything we can to keep South Africa within the Commonwealth. The Commonwealth is not a Commonwealth of Governments but a Commonwealth of peoples —peoples of different racial characteristics.

At the same time, it was our clear duty to see whether there was any way we could influence South Africa to abandon her *apartheid* system.

Now that South Africa has decided to continue her apartheid system and has elected to withdraw from the Commonwealth, it is incumbent on all the members of the Commonwealth and the duty of all nations in the world to bring pressure to bear on South Africa to abandon her apartheid system, imposing total economic and political sanctions on South Africa.

The United Nations should insist on the compliance of South Africa with units Charter obligations. We should insist that South Africa should relinquish its stronghold over South West Africa, a territory which South Africa is supposed to administer a sacred trust of civilisation.

Our sympathy extends to the people of the three High Commission Territories in South Africa. We must do all we can to maintain their independence, to assist them to become examples of racial co-operation and to look forward to their ultimate federation with other independent African states.

7

ON HIS RETURN TO GHANA

AFTER A TRIP TO THE UNITED STATES, THE UNITED KINGDOM AND NORTH AFRICA

Accra
March 24, 1961

J bring you hearty greetings from the many Ghanaians—men and women, your sons and daughters and friends in Britain, in America, in Morocco, and in Tunisia.

It is nearly three weeks now since I left Accra for New York, where I was privileged to address the resumed session of the United Nations Assembly on 7th March.

What I said then must be familiar to you all. I was at pains to make it quite clear to the world Assembly that the problems facing our brothers in the Congo cannot be solved satisfactorily until all Belgian and other foreign interference in that country has been brought to an end.

The attempts of the imperialists and the colonialists to balkanize the African continent in their own interest should be obvious to all except those who refuse to face the realities of what is happening in Africa today.

I put forward to the General Assembly of the United Nations eight practical and in my view, realistic proposals for the solution of the Congo situation.

I am convinced that independent African states, with the support of the Asian and other friendly countries, are of particular importance in the solution of the Congo problem.

While I was in America, I also took the opportunity to call on President Kennedy in Washington, and exchanged views with him on matters concerning Africa and world peace.

I found that the President was most sympathetic with the aims of our African policy, and eager to understand our views.

I was impressed with the obvious sincerity and dynamic approach of his new American administration.

The Commonwealth Conference

This year's Conference of Commonwealth Prime Ministers will go down in history as marking a significant landmark in the affairs of the Commonwealth.

For the first time in its existence, the leaders of the Commonwealth were faced squarely with the challenge of reaffirming their acceptance of the logic of the multi-racial character of the Commonwealth.

The Union of South Africa has decided to withdraw from the Commonwealth rather than abandon or modify the vicious system of apartheid.

There was no alternative but for South Africa to quit the Commonwealth.

South Africa could not have it both ways, maintaining its apartheid system and electing to continue to remain within the Commonwealth.

But as far as we are concerned, this is not the end of the struggle. As I said before leaving London, this is not a struggle between black and white. It is a fight between good and evil; between what is right and what is wrong

In this regard we must do everything possible to mobilise African and world opinion for total economic, political and diplomatic sanctions against South Africa.

I shall very shortly address Parliament on these matters.

Talks in North Africa

During the last two days, I have been visiting Rabat and Tunis, where I have held interesting and fruitful discussions with King Hassan II of Morocco, and President Bourguiba of Tunisia. We were in complete accord in our determination to work for the unity and independence of Africa, and the complete eradication of colonialism in all its forms from this continent.

In Tunisia, I also met Mr. Ferhat Abbas, the leader of the Algerian Provisional Government.

President Bourguiba and I expressed to him our support for his forthcoming negotiations with the French authorities to secure the self-determination and complete independence of Algeria.

We sincerely hope that there will be a new era of peace in Algeria and that the French Government will not impose any conditions which will make a just and peaceful solution impossible.

Thank you all once again. Good luck, and God bless you

NOBLE TASK OF TEACHING

TO THE CONFERENCE OF TEACHERS ASSOCIATION

Legon,
April 6, 1961

I have watched with considerable admiration the steady growth of your various participating associations of science teachers, French teachers, teachers of English and the Conference of Heads of Secondary Schools, and the increasingly good influence which these bodies are exerting on the educational life of this country.

Your decision to hold this session is particularly praiseworthy, in that you as teachers will have the opportunity to see and assess your work in your individual fields and subjects not only in relation to each other's work but also to the whole field of education. I am very glad, therefore, to send you this message and I take this opportunity to congratulate you most warmly on the initiative which you have shown in arranging this function.

It is not my purpose in this message to tell how to conduct yourselves in your profession. My purpose is rather to offer you my encouragement in the pursuit of your noble tasks on which the future of the people of this country so much depends.

The importance of education, especially in developing countries like ours today, cannot be over-emphasised. Education is the firmest foundation of all for any national building process. It is therefore the cornerstone upon which rests our surest hope to build in Ghana a structure of society which will be worthy of a respectable place among the civilised nations of the world.

It is for this reason that my Government attaches the greatest importance to the development of education at all levels. We will spare no efforts to rid this country completely of illiteracy, and banish from it the attendant curses of ignorance, poverty, and disease. It is our aim to ensure that, beginning from primary school level, right through up to university level, there is a continuous flow of talent properly directed to meet our every need, and drawing its inspiration from the challenge to make a definite contribution to world civilisation and culture.

As you know, I recently announced my decision that there should be established as from the 1st September this year a system of free and compulsory primary education. The successful implementation of this system, as well as the whole educational policy of my Government, will depend above all else on the loyalty and co-operation and hard work of all the teachers in this country. A democratic and free country demands not only compulsory and universal primary education but also secondary and higher education for all those who are capable of benefiting from it. It is important that all aspects of our education should be carefully related to the needs of a developing society and geared to the economic, industrial and technological advancement to which we look forward in Ghana.

It is often stated that the purpose of education is to prepare one for life and necessarily for a particular profession or work. In our present circumstances in Ghana it is not enough that anyone should acquire knowledge for its own sake. We are not impressed by the mere acquisition of knowledge. Such knowledge becomes impressive only when it is applied to achieve positive and practical results for the benefit of mankind.

We therefore rely upon you in the course of your works as teachers of the young people of this country to inculcate in them at the same time that spirit of service without which their knowledge, however great, will remain completely barren.

It is the aim of my Government to create gradually a socialist system of society in which every individual will have the greatest opportunity of developing his talents and ability to the utmost. In this society the State will also expect the utmost service from every individual. We rely on on you, headmasters and teachers, to provide and show to the young people and students of Ghana a worthy example of this spirit of service. We have every right to expect that the students under you should by your example identify themselves with the political and economic aspirations of the people of Ghana.

We are now entering an era of rapid scientific, economic and technological development in Ghana. It is no secret that it is the aim of my Government that this country should be industrialised as soon as possible as a complement to our agricultural development. We realise, however, that the achievement of this aim will be dependent in large measure on the speed with which our educational system can turn out the men and women who will be required for the implementation of our projects. I refer here also to the lack of an adequate supply of qualified students to our institutions of higher learning. This difficulty has been brought to our notice by the Commission on University Education which was recently appointed by the Government. In view of the importance which the Government attaches to this matter. I have decided to appoint a commission as soon as possible to examine the entire structure of education in Ghana. It is hoped that this commission will be composed of educationists who have had experience of educational development in areas of rapid social, economic and technological change.

It is well known that education in Ghana has been considerably expanded within the last ten years. During this period we have tried to adapt the educational system to meet the rapid changes taking place in our country. The provision of full sixth form facilities, the introduction of French as a compulsory subject in secondary schools, and the increasing bias in the secondary school curriculum towards science, mathematics and allied subjects, have all been carried out in accordance with this policy. But much more remains to be done.

It is necessary that technical courses should be provided at all levels in addition to the "grammar school" type of course which now exists. We need in fact to expand at all levels. At the primary level we have to aim at a completely literate working population. We need to expand the teacher training system to provide the teachers for universal education. We need also to expand the secondary school system itself to feed our universities continuously. Facilities for technical education should be extended so that our industrialisation can move forward without over-dependence on imported skills. We need finally to expand and adapt our university system to provide a greater variety of courses which will have relevance to the needs of our country.

As an illustration of what measures the Government is taking to meet these needs, training colleges, for instance, have been asked to increase their enrolment by various method, and day training colleges will be opened shortly. In accordance with the gigantic Second Development Plan launched by the Convention People's Party Government two years ago, new secondary schools have been established throughout the country.

The Ghana Educational Trust which I established to build Ghana schools and colleges is doing magnificent work. The Trust has so far built thirteen new secondary schools, has rehoused five others, and will be opening eight more in September this year. As a result largely of the work of this body, the number of secondary schools within the public system has risen from 39 in 1960 to 59. The annual increase in pupil intake to forms one and two has been most encouraging, and is now well over 4,000.

The Government is fully aware of the extra burdens and the difficulties in staffing which this expansion has brought in its train. Your problems about qualified staff, particularly in science, mathematics and French, are well known to me, and my Government is taking the necessary steps to remedy the situation.

I am pleased to say that as an indication of the value and importance which my Government attaches to associations such as yours, it has been decided that the sum of £G1,000 should be provided for you next year to assist your associations.

Finally, I wish to assure you of my Government's appreciation of the vital role which you have played in the development of Ghana and to express the hope that we can continue to rely on your co-operation and advice in the exciting task of developing Ghana. I congratulate you again for arranging this conference and I wish you success in your deliberations.

9

DAWN BROADCAST

April 8, 1961

GOOD MORNING, FRIENDS AND COUNTRYMEN,

In accordance with the cherished customs of our fathers, whereby advice is sought or given at early dawn, I have come to the microphone this early morning to share some thoughts with you in a homely chat.

Four years ago we achieved independence and set out on a new road to nationhood. On the 1st of July, 1960, we consolidated this political achievement by setting up the Republic as an expansion of our sovereign will. That day marked the real beginning of life of our nation and settled upon us responsibility not only for the development and reconstruction of Ghana, but also for the faithful duty of assisting other African territories to achieve their freedom and independence.

This responsibility casts upon all Ghanaians an obligation to protect the national stability we have so ably created and to guard ever jealously the solidarity of our nation. For this reason I have been rather unhappy about reports which I have received since my return from the United Kingdom; and this has led me to speak to you this morning, to examine the matters forming the subject of these reports, and to discuss them openly and sincerely.

When I was away certain matters arose concerning the Trades Union Congress, the National Assembly, the Co-operative Movement and the United Ghana Farmers Council. These matters created misunderstandings and led to some regrettable demonstrations.

I do not think that this stage of our national life, when all our efforts should be concentrated upon building a first-class nation, we should allow petty misunderstandings and squabbles to divert our attention from our great and worthy aims and objectives.

What was the cause of these unfortunate circumstances? Some Parliamentarians criticised the Trades Union Congress and the other wing organisations of the Convention People's Party. The officials of these organisations objected to the criticism and made counter-criticisms against certain Parliamentarians and this started a vicious circle of criminations and recriminations. This is clearly unfortunate. I have taken certain steps, and I hope that no occasion will arise to cause a recurrence of a similar situation.

The Convention People's Party a is great brotherhood. Its strength is embedded in the unity of its membership and since both sides to this unfortunate dispute are members of the Convention People's Party, I wish to examine the situation and look deeper for the causes of this incident.

I have stated over and over again, that members of the Convention People's Party must not use their party membership or official position for personal gain or for the amassing of wealth. Such tendencies directly contradict our party constitution, which makes it clear that the aims and objects of the party, among other things, are the building of a socialist pattern of society in which the free development of each is the condition for the free development of all—a pattern or society consonant with Africa situations, circumstances and conditions.

I have explained very clearly this socialist structure and have on many occasions elaborated the five sectors into which our economy may be divided. These sectors are: first, the state sector, in which all enterprises are entirely state-owned; second, the joint state-private sector, which will incorporate enterprises owned jointly by Government and foreign private capital, third, the co-operative sector, in which all enterprises will be undertaken by co-operative organisations affiliated with the National Co-operative Council, fourth, the private enterprises sector, which will incorporate those industries which are open freely to foreign private enterprise, and fifth, the workers' enterprise sector.

I have had occasions to emphasise the part which private enterprise will continue to play in our economic and industrial life. A different situation arises with Ghanaian businessmen who attempt to combine business with political life. Being a party Member of the Assembly—and much more, being a Ministerial Secretary or a Minister—means that the persons who take up these positions owe a duty to those who have elected them or who have given them their positions with confidence. To be able to maintain this confidence, therefore, they should not enter into any type of industrial or commercial undertaking. Any party member of Parliament who wishes to be a businessman can do so, but he should give up his seat in Parliament. In other words, no Minister, Ministerial Secretary or party Member of Parliament should own a business or be involved in anyone else's business, Ghanaian or foreign.

In spite of my constant clarifications and explanations of our aims and objectives, some party Members in Parliament pursue a course of conduct in direct contradiction of our party aims. They are tending, by virtue of their functions and positions, to become a separate social group aiming to become a new ruling class of self-seeking and careerists. This tendency is working to alienate the support of the masses and to bring the National Assembly into isolation.

Members of Parliament must remember at all times that they are representatives of their constituencies only by reason of their party membership and that on no account should they regard party constituency representation as belonging to them in their own right. In other words, constituencies are not the property of Members of Parliament. It is the party that sends them there and fights for them to become Members of Parliament. I am sure that from now on all Parliamentarians will be guided accordingly in their conduct of representing the party in Parliament.

When I look at the other side of the picture, I must say that some Trades Union officials have now and again indulged in loose talk and reprehensible statements which do no good either to the party, to the Government or to the nation. This is not the time for unbridled militant trade unionism in our country. Trade union officials must shed their colonial character and their colonial thinking. The approach of the Trades Union Congress to our national issues should be reasoned and constructive in accordance with our present circumstances.

Let me now turn to some other causes which I consider plague Ghanaian society generally and militate against undisturbed progress. A great deal of rumour-mongering goes on all over the country.

"Berko said that the Odikro informed Asamani that the Ohene said he paid a sum of money to a party official to become a paramount chief."

"Kojo said that Mensah told him that Kweku took a bribe."

"Abena stated that Ekua said Esi uses her relations with Kweku to get contracts through the District Commissioner with the support of the Regional Commissioner and the blessing of a minister in Accra."

So, day and day, night after night, all types and manner of wild allegations and rumours are circulated and they are always well sprinkled with: *they say, they say, wosee, wosee, akee, akee!*

Many members of the party and of the public are guilty of this conduct. I have directed that in future, any allegations or rumours so made or circulated against any person must immediately be brought before the central committee of the party for investigation.

One of the most degrading aspects of party conducts is the tendency on the part of some comrades to go round using the names of persons in prominent positions to collect money for themselves. Equally degrading is the tendency on the part of some persons in prominent positions to create agents for collecting money. This is a shameful and highly criminal tendency which must be crushed in the most ruthless manner.

May I take this opportunity to stress an essential point. Statements which may be regarded as Government policy are those which are clearly stated in the text to be the official policy of the Government.

In recent months people in Ghana and abroad have frequently been confused and the Government's policies made uncertain as a result of unauthorised statements which have been made by persons employed by the Government, or quasi-Government bodies. Often these statements have conflicted with the Government's policies, and although they have been corrected subsequently by the Government, much harm has been done, and confusion and suspicion have resulted.

In spite of the freedom of speech which can reasonably be allowed in such cases, I consider that firm action should in the national interest, be taken. From now on, therefore no public statement affecting Government policy will be made by any Minister, Ministerial Secretary, member of a Government cooperation or institution, Government official or any other person employed by the Government, unless that statement has first had Presidential or Cabinet approval. It is my intention to take strong disciplinary action against any individual who infringes this procedure.

I am aware that the evil of patronage finds a good deal of place in our society. I consider that it is entirely wrong for persons placed in positions of eminence or authority to use the influence of office in patronising others, in many cases wrong persons, for immoral favours. I am seeing to it that this evil shall be uprooted, no matter whose ox is gored. The same thing goes for nepotism, which is, so to speak, a twin brother of the evil of patronage.

At this point, I would like to make a little divergence and touch upon Civil Service red tape. It amazes me that up to the present many civil servants do not realise that we are living in a revolutionary era. This Ghana, which has lost so much time serving colonial masters, cannot afford to be tied down to archaic snail-pace methods of work which obstruct expeditious progress. We have lost so much time that we need to do in ten years what has taken others a hundred years to accomplish. Civil servants, therefore, must develop a new orientation, a sense of mission and urgency to enable them to eliminate all tendencies towards red tape-ism, bureaucracy and waste. Civil servants must use their initiative to make the Civil Service an effective instrument in the rapid development of Ghana.

In order to promote greater efficiency in the machinery of the Government, I have decided to re-organise slightly the existing ministerial set-up. In view of the increasingly important part being played by Ghana at the present time in the African liberation movement I have decided to create a Ministry of African Affairs, as distinct from the present Ministry of Foreign Affairs. This new

Ministry will be responsible for all African matters, including the present duties undertaken by the Bureau of African Affairs and the African Affairs Centre. It will also liaise with the All-African People's Secretariat and the All-African Trade Union Federation.

The Ministry of Labour and Co-operatives and Ministry of Social Welfare will be abolished. Ministerial responsibility for labour, social welfare and community development matters will be undertaken by the Ministry of Education, which will therefore be known as the Ministry of Education, Labour and Social Welfare. The staff of the Co-operative Department will be seconded to the National Co-operative Council to assist the council in the supervision and co-ordination of co-operative activities throughout the country.

Responsibility for consumer co-operatives, agricultural co-operatives and industrial co-operatives will be undertaken by the Ministry of Trade, the Ministry of Agriculture and the Development Secretariat, respectively.

Let me say a few words about the purchase of cocoa. The report I have received so far indicate that the statement made in Parliament some time ago by the Minister of Labour and Co-operatives, that a state buying agency would be established by the Government and that this agency would control the purchase of cocoa throughout the country, has not been favourably received by the farmers. After careful consideration, I have come to the conclusion that this proposal, which was announced to Parliament, is perhaps not the best way in which we can handle this important matter of the purchase of cocoa. It is of the utmost importance that the arrangements for the purchase of our cocoa, which is not only the source of livelihood for the majority of people in this country but also of such utmost importance to our economy, should be as simple and efficient as possible. I have therefore instructed that the United Ghana Farmers' Council, which embraces all the farmers of Ghana, should be given the sole responsibility for organising the purchase of all cocoa produced in Ghana on behalf of the Cocoa Marketing Board.

I am assured by the United Ghana Farmers' Council that they have made all the necessary arrangements and are prepared to undertake the purchase of cocoa as from the main crop season this year.

A satisfactory safeguard in respect of this matter has been provided in an arrangement which I have directed for the auditing of the accounts of the United Ghana Farmers' Council by the Auditor-General. By this arrangement the accounts of the United Ghana Farmers' Council, all public corporations, the Trades Union Congress and all other bodies concerned shall be audited by the Auditor-General who shall have the same powers in relation to them as are conferred upon him by the Constitution in relation to Government accounts.

As I said at the recent civic luncheon arranged in my honour at the Ambassador Hotel by the Accra City Council, I am very anxious that the city of Accra should be developed as quickly as possible in view of its increasing international importance. In order to speed up this process, I have appointed a Special Commissioner for Accra Development, who will be responsible to me, through the Minister of Works and Housing for the rapid implementation of all public works in respect of the city of Accra and the general development of the city.

In particular, he will be concerned with the development within the city of Accra of parks, children's playgrounds, public swimming pools and other such amenities, and also with the construction of streets and slum clearance schemes and of a sewerage system. I trust that the Special Commissioner will receive the full co-operation of the Accra City Council and the people of Accra in this most important assignment.

I have recently been alarmed at the amount of travelling abroad which is undertaken by Ministers, ambassadors, Ministerial Secretaries and civil servants of all ranks. In many cases it is clear that approval is sought from no one before the journeys concerned are made. In future, travelling abroad unless approved by the Cabinet, will not be paid for by the Government. The cost of any journeys which are undertaken without this approval will be surcharged to the person concerned. I have also directed that instructions should be given to the heads of all public boards and corporations, to ensure that no officers of these boards and corporations travel outside Ghana at Government expense without my specific approval or that of the Cabinet.

Ghanaian Ambassadors take their children with them when they proceed to their stations, at the expense of the Government. I am taking steps to discourage this practice for it seems to me that on psychological and other grounds, it is better for those young children to begin their education at home.

At any rate this practice cannot be justified on financial grounds. In future, Ambassadors and foreign service officers will not be allowed to take their children abroad unless such children are below the age of five years. The procedure will apply equally to civil servants and other Ghanaian public functionaries serving abroad.

Let me now come back to the party.

It is most important to remember that the strength of the Convention People's Party derives from the masses of the people. These men and women include those whom I have constantly referred to as the unknown warriors—dedicated men and women who serve the party loyally and selflessly without hoping for reward. It is therefore natural for the masses to feel some resentment when they see comrades whom they have put into power and given the mandate to serve the country on their behalf, begin to forget themselves and indulge in ostentatious living. High party officials, Ministers, Ministerial Secretaries, chairmen of statutory boards and corporations must forever bear this in mind. Some of us very easily forget that we ourselves have risen from amongst the masses. We must avoid any conduct that will breed antagonism and uneasy relations. Let us always keep in mind the fact that constant examination and correction are necessary for maintaining the solidarity of the the party. The aim of all correction, however, must be to build and not to destroy. The central committee proposes to issue instructions shortly on the duties and rights of party members.

Coming to the integral organisations of the party, I consider it essential to emphasise once more that the Trades Union Congress, the United Ghana Farmers' Council, the National Co-operative Council and the National Council of Ghana Women, are integral parts of the Convention People's Party, and in order to correct certain existing anomalies, the central committee has decided that separate membership cards of the integral organisations shall be abolished forthwith. The membership card of the party will be only qualifications for membership within these organisations, namely, the Trades Union Congress, the United Ghana Farmers' Council, the National Co-operative Council and the National Council of Ghana Women, and no other membership card other than that of the Convention People's Party shall be recognised by these bodies. In all regional headquarters, provision will be made for the central party and these integral organisations to be housed in one building. This is necessary for effective co-ordination and control. Also the separate flags used by these organisations will be abolished and replaced by the flag of the Convention People's Party.

At his stage, I wish to take the opportunity to refer to an internal matter of the Trades Union Congress. It has come to my notice that dues of 4s. per month are being paid by some unions, whereas others pay 2s. monthly as membership dues. I understand that this position is causing some irritation. I have therefore instructed, after consultation with the Trades Union Congress officials, that union dues shall remain at 2s. per month.

Finally, I wish to state that in considering remedial measures, I have found it necessary to direct that a limit be imposed on property acquisition by Ministers, party officials and Ministerial Secretaries in order to enable them to conform to the modest and simple way of life demanded by the ideals and principles of the Convention People's Party.

Countrymen: Our mission to Ghana and to Africa and the unique personality of our party as a vanguard of the African liberation movement impose upon us increasing responsibility not only to set our own house in order, but also to set very high standards from which all who seek to emulate us shall draw devotion and inspiration in their own struggles.

I wish you all good luck and a good week-end.

10

AFRICA MUST BE FREE

AFRICA FREEDOM DAY
April 15, 1961

On the occasion of the third anniversary of Africa Freedom Day I am happy to send you this message.

The continued struggle of Africans and peoples of African descent against centuries of imperialist domination and colonialist exploitation, and for their right to freedom and independence, has been a peculiarly difficult one; it has nevertheless been carried out relentlessly and with ever-increasing determination and strength. To-day, on our great continent of Africa, we find the evil forces of colonialism and imperialism on the retreat.

It is true that in this bitter struggle we have achieved successes unprecedented in the annals of colonial history. We should, however, never allow ourselves to be deceived into a state of passive complacency. There are living millions of Africans languishing in colonial bondage and living in the most wretched conditions in many parts of this continent. The revival of colonialism in the Congo is sufficient evidence and warning of the treacherous character of imperialism and its menace even to independent states and of the danger of the new colonialism which is more subtle but equally vicious.

We in Ghana regard our independence as meaningless unless it is closely linked up with the total liberation of Africa. Together with our brothers, we are carrying on the struggle for the liberation and unity of Africa and shall continue in this struggle until every inch of African soil has been liberated and every vestige of colonial oppression and suppression has been eliminated.

The destiny of Africans everywhere is inseparably linked by our common heritage, common ideals and aspirations. It develops upon all African leaders, and the leaders of people of African descent, to unite in pursuit of our common objective—the total liberation of

Africa and the union of independent African states. Only in this way can we constitute ourselves into a force sufficiently formidable to crush colonialism and imperialism utterly and completely from the face of this continent.

I send warm greetings and fraternal good wishes to all African freedom fighters everywhere. Let them rededicate themselves to this worthy cause and let them remember all the time that as long as any part of Africa remains unfree, the struggle continues.

11

BUILDING A SOCIALIST STATE

TO THE C. P. P. STUDY GROUP

Accra,
April, 22, 1961

COMRADES AND FRIENDS,

The paramount task before us and the nation is the raising of an equitable and progressive social order which will provide food, clothing and shelter to meet the needs of the people in accordance with their means; a social order that will reflect a higher standard of living in the happiness of our people.

Economically, this means full employment, good housing and equal opportunity for educational and cultural advancement up to the highest level possible for all the people. In concrete facts, it means:

> that the real income of all types of workers, farmers and peasants must rise;
>
> that prices of goods must not over-leap wages;
>
> that house rentals must be within the means of all groups;
>
> that educational and cultural amenities must be available to all people.

If ability to pay is the passport to the good life, then at this time most of the people of this country are precluded from it. And unless we, the leaders of the party of the people, make good our economic and social programme, then they are doomed to perpetual exclusion from the good life and the purpose of our effort is defeated.

This is the tremendous task not of the Convention People's Party alone, but of the whole nation; civil servants, all types of workers, teachers, farmers, peasants—indeed, all able-bodied Ghanaians standing together as one man under the leadership of the Convention People's Party. The question then is: how are we to achieve this goal within the shortest possible time?

As our party has proclaimed, and as I have asserted time and again, socialism is the only pattern that can within the shortest possible time bring the good life to the people. For socialism assumes the public ownership of the means of production—the land and its resources—and the use of those means for production that will bring benefit to the people. Socialist production is production of goods and services in fulfilment of the people's needs. It is not production for individual private profit, which deprives such a large section of the people of the goods, and services produced, while their needs and wants remain unsatisfied.

One point, however, we have to get clear. At this juncture, Ghana is not a socialist state. Not only do the people as yet not own all the major means of production and distribution, but we have still to lay the actual foundations upon which socialism can be built, namely, the complete industrialisation of our country. All talk of socialism, of economic and social reconstruction, are just empty words if we do not seriously address ourselves to the question of basic industrialisation and agricultural revolution in our country, just as mush as we must concentrate on socialist education.

Secondary industries are vitally necessary, for it is one of our principal aims to replace imports of foreign goods by home-produced goods. Moreover, secondary industries must be planned to take up the production of our agriculture and to widen the outlets for the output of our farmers and peasants. But secondary industries, important as they are to making us economically independent, will still leave us heavily reliant upon outside sources and skill unless we build up those heavy industries which alone provide the fundamental basis of industrialisation.

Such projects as the steel-producing plant, the oil refinery and the machine tool plant which we are planning, as well as the Volta and Bui electrification schemes, are capital projects in the real sense of the term. Energy is an indispensable element in industrialisation. Without energy—without coal, oil or hydro-electricity—it is idle to talk of industrialisation. Without energy we cannot lay the foundations of industrialisation. Industrialisation presupposes electrification. Indeed, it is our lack of vital sources of energy that has been preventing us from carrying into effect so many of our ideas and plans for our national reconstruction. We could not even talk about a steel plant until we could envisage energy for working it.

Hence my preoccupation with the Volta River Project and other schemes that will provide water power both for electricity and irrigation of regions that are starved of water at certain periods of the year. These schemes and projects are an essential key to our industrial progress, the basis upon which we may build up our heavy industries, our machine-tool factories and our ancillary manufactures. As long as we are unable to make our own machine tools, the instruments for the manufacture of all the myriad commodities, large and small, that we at present import, we shall continue to be at the mercy of outside sources of supply. We shall continue to be economically dependent and all talk of socialist progress will be so much empty chatter.

To implement our objective of basic economic reconstruction, we must henceforth earmark a much larger proportion of our national revenue to the erection of basic industries and the multiplication of our agricultural products. We must try and establish factories in large numbers at great speed and see to it that there is quick development of electricity and water supplies.

And here a revolution is needed in our approach to planning. Unfortunately, our planning hitherto has largely been piecemeal and unpurposeful. It has not been linked in an organised manner. Too many government and semi-governmental bodies and departments have been concerned in the drawing up and executing of plans. What we need are not reports but plans of action. Too often the relation of these bodies and departments with each other and with the different sectors of the national economy has been unco-ordinated. As a result there has been much wastage of precious funds and limited managerial and technical staff. Planning, moreover, has been seen principally from Accra, and in the main, the obvious national projects have not received attention.

Our planning, if it is to revitalise the country, increase our productivity and progress towards our socialist objective, must spread out into all corners of the country. It must take stock of all our human and natural resources, it must count our economic assets, We must make an inventory of our natural, mineral and agricultural heritage, we must number our man-power and our actual and potential reservoir of skills.

Only thus can we plan for our total development at all levels of our national life.

This means that everything we do must be related to our overall plan. Educational, social welfare and health programmes, for example, cannot be devised in isolation. They must be planned in relation to the needs of our healthy development and the enhancement of the lives of the people. Plans for these sectors must be coordinated with our plans for the economic sphere. For our economic expansion will need urgently the output of the schools, the technical institutes and universities.

Above all, our objective of economic advancement is seen as the foundation upon which to erect an equitable and happy society. Hence our planning cannot be restricted to the main centres of the country. It must stretch out into the regions. It is my intention to constitute the regional divisions of the country into economic units, with the local councils as economic sub-units. These units will henceforth consider increased production (in the factories, the farms, the offices, the homes, and so forth) as their first concern, alongside the maintenance of law and order

Our planning must eliminate the sorry plight of students—boys and girls leaving school and roaming about the country—who gravitate towards Accra and other big towns in search of work and who, when they cannot get work, fall into bad ways. I am of the opinion that this problem can best be tackled by the local authorities with the assistance of the central government. This phase of planning, therefore will be primarily the concern of the local councils and the regional organisations. But these local plans must necessarily fit into full scope of the national planning.

Thus there will be planning at all levels—national, regional and local.

Our central planning organisation will correlate all this planning and set annual targets of achievement. These targets will embrace not only output and the absorption of planned numbers of workers in the different categories; they must arrange for the training of skills and management for the planned projects. They will include estimated margins for industrial expansion, for maintenance and renewals of machinery and equipment.

There will have to be the strictest control against the overspeeding of allocations on given projects so that they may not be called to a standstill for lack of funds to complete them. We are all aware of the shocking disregard for and misuse of public funds and property that presently obtains, especially in such departments as the public works and the transport services. Our new economic and industrial policy, which will give priority to heavy industry alongside the extension of light industries, electricity and water supplies, will have to control severely our financial budgets.

These budgets must be closely integrated, as they must cover every phase of the national planning. Our present budgetary system, which has been taken over from the colonial regime, calls for adjustment to the socialist objective of our planning. Hitherto, our budgeting has been done separately by each department of the state administration. This approach has related projects to the ideas of each different department.

A totally new approach is needed, which will see the national objective of our planning and break it down for implementation by the departments which will be concerned with the fulfilment of its different aspects. They will then be allocated the budget required for their part of the planning.

Our planning must aim at a two-fold purpose: to increase productivity and to accumulate capital for the expansion of industrialisation. Under the new policy, development must be financed more and more from production, which must be targeted, and less and less from taxes and dues, which make heavy demands of these sections of the community least able to afford them. I anxiously look forward to the day when there will be no more personal taxation in the country. Only increased productivity can give surpluses for re-investment in further production and in this way increase our real wealth.

To raise wages without securing a higher rate of productivity is to set in motion the vicious circle of a greater volume of money chasing scarce goods and resulting in inflation. Increased productivity, coupled with socialist planning, will permit the control of prices and the circulation of goods in the community interests. It does not mean that every advance in productivity will lead to an immediate enhancement of standards of living. This is especially the case in the early stages of industrialisation, when the need to plough back capital achieved out of greater productivity is of paramount importance more to the strengthening of the economic base than to consumer goods.

The socialist objective implies the over-all good of the nation, and in the interests of that socialist objective it may be necessary for all of us to forego some small immediate personal benefit for a greater benefit a bit later on. Social services in the interest of the community for instance, confer more advantages upon a greater number than would increased wages for certain groups of workers. But as productivity rises appreciably and the socialist base of the economy extends through the increasing public ownership of the means of production—the land and its natural resources, the factories and their production—a government can not only mobilise greater surpluses of capital in the best interests of the country, but can also reach a position from which it can reward labour for its greater exertions by increased wages. And because the government, through its planning, can at the same time operate controls upon commodity prices, labour will feel a double benefit in a wage increase which will not be eaten up in higher prices as under a capitalist economy.

If our new economic and industrial policy is to succeed, then there must be a change of outlook in those who are responsible for running of affairs. They must acquire a socialist perspective and a socialist drive keyed to the national needs and demands, and not remain the servants of a limping bureaucracy. The executives of our public and statutory organisations must achieve a new attitude to their jobs, which they owe to the struggles of the people and the labour of the farmers and workers. Too many of the Industrial Development Corporation and agricultural Development Corporation projects are at present being subsidised instead of producing profit for further capital investment. This state of affairs must be reversed or the projects closed down. The Industrial Development Corporation must concentrate on basic and secondary industries— real industries that stimulate and promote the utilisation of the productive resources of our country.

For no economy, least of all a young one like ours, struggling to find a stable economic base, can afford to drain its resources in subsidising unproductive ventures from which only well-paid executives profit. Moreover, we cannot afford to waste our resources in men and materials in this way, but must use them wisely in pursuit of our aim of socialist benefits for all the people.

Here it is that our great party must once more take the lead, by educating our men of affairs in their responsibilities to the nation in the conduct of the establishments to which they have been assigned. And just as political independence could not have been attained without the leadership of the Convention People's Party, so Ghana's economic independence and the objective of socialism will not be achieved without the unique leadership of our party, in the fullest and most active co-operation with the people.

Our party must be the pivot of our economic planning, and so henceforth the following procedure will be adopted:

(1) The chairman of the central committee shall be responsible for presenting the main principles and outline of any plan for the central committee's approval.

(2) The principles and outlined programme approved by the central committee shall be referred to the Economic and Planning Secretariat, where it shall be subject to expert examination.

(3) The proposals shall then be submitted to the Cabinet through the standing development committee.

(4) Parliamentary examination and approval will follow.

(5) The final stage will now have been reached, that of putting the plan into execution through all the agencies and communities concerned, and especially through the active leadership of the party.

This procedure should secure the best consultation with and participation of the people. For we shall at all stages seek the co-operation of all the people and organisations who are to be concerned, in the final analysis, in performing the basic work that will make success of such a plan. It is only with the wholehearted interest and support of the mass of the people in the carrying out of any such plan, that such a plan can succeed.

It is for these reasons that I am convinced that the procedure I have outlined, with all it implies in mass consultations, is our surest way to success. There will be an evolving ascendancy of popular control of the country's affairs which, in effect, will be the trust kind of democracy that has ever functioned. For it will realise the aim of bringing most of the people into the running of the nation's affairs, in the interests of the people. It will, in effect, be placing government in the hands of the people, to be run for the people by the people.

Control of the modern state is linked up with the control of the means of production.

True democracy can be said to exist only when the majority of the people exercise control of the state in the interests of all the people, because the means of production and distribution have passed into its hands. In other words, the general will of the people, which is the most concrete and the clearest expression of true democracy, must be actively asserted.

To attain this laudable end of socialist control we have from time to time to make a review of the administrative apparatus at our disposal, remembering that it was originally bequeathed to us by a colonial regime dedicated to a very different purpose. Even through this apparatus has already been subjected to considerable changes, it still carries vestiges of inherited attitudes and ways of thought which have been transmitted even to some of our newer institutions. In our adaptations, because we are embarking upon an uncharted path we may have to proceed from trial and error. Changes which are made to-day may themselves call for further change tomorrow. But when we are endeavouring to establish a new kind of life within a kind of society, we must acknowledge the fact that we are in a period of flux and cannot afford to be hide-bound in our decisions and attitudes. We must accommodate our minds and attitudes to the need for constant adaptation.

The new drive for economic and industrial development has necessitated some reorganisation in the ministerial structure of the government. From what I have been saying, it is obvious that planning must have its due emphasis. The chief agencies for mobilising capital for development will be the Industrial Development Corporation (for state industries) and the Agricultural Development Corporation (for state farms), and the role of these statutory bodies needs drastic revision. At present, as I have said earlier on, they work on projects in a haphazard manner. From now on, they must cease their isolated approach and work according to the new economic policy which I have outlined.

The Industrial Development Corporation will therefore come under the direct control of the Development Secretariat, and the Agricultural Development Corporation under the Minister of Agriculture.

In discussing the role of the Industrial Development Corporation and the Agricultural Development Corporation in the new economic and industrial drive, it is only appropriate that we should deal with the National Co-operative Council, which has some functions similar to those of the corporations. Briefly, the National Co-operative Council has four main functions, namely: industrial development, agricultural development, or consumer development and development of welfare services and the co-operative spirit.

I have recently made the following adjustments as a means of facilitating the efficient operation of the co-operative movement:

(1) The National Co-operative Council, as the supreme co-operative body, shall be charged with the general functions of co-ordination and supervision, as well as the promotion of the co-operative spirit, that is, the dissemination of co-operative education and development. It will also be charged with the authority to represent the co-operative at home and abroad. In the performance of this function it will act in co-operation with the appropriate apex body, according to the kind of representation required.

(2) The National Co-operative Council will maintain contract with the ministry responsible for social welfare and the Labour Secretariat in regard to the provision of welfare services for members of the co-operative.

(3) The industrial co-operative, generally known as Indusco, will deal with the Development Secretariat, which is responsible for industrial development.

(4) The agricultural co-operative will deal with the Ministry of Agriculture.

(5) The consumer co-operative will deal with the Ministry of Trade, which will be responsible for the National Trading Corporation when it is set up.

(6) I have established under the Auditor-General an accounting and auditing service also which will take away the main functions of the Department of Co-operation. The department as such will thus cease to exist, as its other functions, such as co-operative development and education, will be taken over by the National Co-

operative Council. In view of the importance of safeguarding public funds, I have charged this auditing and accounting service with the responsibility of looking after the funds of the Trades Union Congress, the United Ghana Farmers' Council and the statutory boards and corporations.

In this economic and industrial exercise, we shall need trained men and women in great numbers. The government has therefore decreed that free and compulsory primary and middle school education should be started from September next, and that the whole country should be literate by the time we celebrate the 10th anniversary of our Republic.

The recent commission on higher education that I set up has reported and the recommendations are being urgently examined for early implementation. In the meantime, I have the following observations and recommendations to make.

The Academy of Learning should be given a more positive and active role than it has at the moment, and this should be reflected in a change of the name to The Ghana Academy of Sciences. The most important role of the Ghana Academy of Sciences will be research into the sciences, history, language, etc. It should be the body to plan research for the country and should thus absorb the National Research Council. Duplication and overlapping of effort would thereby be avoid and this would eliminate the restriction to a learned body.

The new National Council for Higher Education and Research will therefore have two wings:

(1) universities, and (2) The Ghana Academy of Sciences; while its proper functions will be: (a) To make policy; (b) To approve plans and programmes; (c) To co-ordinate efforts; and (d) To provide grants, etc

There has been some hesitation in the establishment of research institutes. These loom in importance as the need for industrial and technological development presses, and I think concentrated effort and drive are now called for in setting them up. Foreign specialists will, in the initial stages, be required for a time to do the research work, but I feel that we must try and appoint as many Ghanaians as possible to administer them.

In my view, the staff and personnel of the institutes and universities should be interchangeable, and these various bodies should work together with each other and with the factories, farms, administrations, laboratories, and so on connected with their work. As far as possible we should seek native talent in the field and in institutions, both locally and overseas, to man the universities and scientific institutions, since they must now take their place in the forefront of the production drive. Priority in the assignment of trained personnel should be given to these organisations, and it should be a matter of national pride to work in them.

Indeed there are many problems for the solution of which we must look to our scientific institutions. For instance, with more and more cocoa coming to glut the market, the West African Cocoa Research Institute should not lose any time in setting up a commercial department for dealing with cocoa derivatives.

We have, too, many species of timber that are not being used. This is a complete waste and the timber utilisation research unit should be turned into a proper institute, adequately manned so that it can cope with the problem and give effective results.

The location of the various institutes is a matter for the National Council for Higher Education and Research, though proposals will be submitted for decision by the Ghana Academy of Sciences.

I would like to emphasis that at this time the annual meeting and report of the Ghana Academy of Sciences are matters of national importance, for they record progress and outline plans for future work. The title of Academician should be recognised as one of the highest national awards.

With this new approach to our economic and industrial development, every avenue of information and education must be used to stir the political consciousness of the people and to make them alive to the objectives of the government's planning. I have already said that without the support of the masses of the people, our plans can fail. The people need to be stirred to a new awareness of their role in carrying forward our national reconstruction. They must be refreshed in the plans which swept them into the battle for political emancipation that brought them independence.

The party cadres, who must be in the forefront of the educational drive, must reinforce their own understanding through party political education. Many of our ministers, party officials, ministerial secretaries, heads of boards and corporations, Members of Parliament and journalists, able men as they are, and party members, are yet without a socialist understanding and orientation.

Now that the party school at Winneba is ready, a start must be made to alter this position, and we should, without delay, start from the top. I am therefore directing that:

(1) Members of the central committee, ministers and regional commissioners and general secretaries of subsidiary bodies of the party shall attend a one week's residential course at Winneba. I shall be there myself to conduct it.

(2) The next group shall include ministerial secretaries, chairmen of boards and corporations, headquarters secretaries of the bureau of the party, the T.U.C., etc

(3) A third group will consist of backbenchers, regional officers of the party and of subsidiary organisations. Other individuals may be added to the various groups as may be considered desirable. The ordinary training of cadres will then resume, the course being much longer.

We cannot build socialism without socialists and we must take positive steps to ensure that the party and the country produce men and women who can handle a socialist programme. The analysis of our economic and industrial policy imposes upon all civil servants and public functionaries an urgent duty to put their work their very, very best. If there are some executives, whether they be expatriates or Ghanaians who would obstruct and pull us back instead of pushing us forward, then they must be honest enough to quit their posts bag and baggage.

Comrades, I have outlined to you the new economic and industrial policy for ushering in a new era in Ghana. We are just at the beginning and much, indeed, remains to be done. We have set our machinery for effective action, and certain steps must be taken without any delay.

Friends and Comrades, Africa needs a new type of man; a dedicated, modest, honest and devoted man. A man who submerges self in service to his nation and mankind. A man who abhors greed and detests vanity. A new type of man whose meekness is his strength and whose integrity is his greatness. Africa's new man must be a man indeed.

All this needs a great deal of zeal. Let us remember, however, that our zeal should make us adroit and alert to all the implications of our actions. For we have a tremendous, Herculean task before us. It needs all our care, all our brains. Our party, through all its members, must show its merits in this our greatest mission yet—the building of a socialist Ghana. This mission you must discharge with responsibility and integrity.

12
THE FIGHT ON TWO FRONTS

ON ASSUMPTION OF OFFICE AS GENERAL SECRETARY AND CHAIRMAN OF THE CENTRAL COMMITTEE OF THE C. P.P.

May 1, 1961

COMRADES AND FRIENDS,

This morning I assumed duty as General Secretary of the party and chairman of the central committee. I have done so at the request of the Central Committee because we have entered a new phase: Firstly, even though our political revolution is over, we are entering into a new political revolution with regard to the struggle for the total liberation and unity of Africa. And, secondly, at home we have entered a new phase of industrial and technological revolution, and the whole country must be mobilised for the realisation of these two objectives. As general secretary it is my responsibility to give personal and executive direction to the party and to the government and to make sure that our forces are properly developed to give victory in this most important exercise. Incidentally, this day is also May Day—the international workers day, and I take this opportunity to send greetings to workers throughout the world, and particularly to the workers of Ghana and of Africa.

This arrangement whereby I have taken over the General Secretaryship of the party, has necessitated some administrative changes at party headquarters, as a result of which the following appointments have been made: Comrade H. H. C. Crabbe has been appointed Chief Administrative Officer and Comrade A. A. Adjaye has been appointed District Commissioner for Accra in his place. Comrades J. K. Bonsu, K. S. Annan (formerly Assistant General Secretaries) and Comrade A. G. Quartey, former District Commissioner, Krachi, have been appointed Deputy Chief Administrative officers.

Comrade A.Y. K Djin has been appointed National Treasurer and Comrade N. A. Welbeck as liaison officer. Comrade G. Y. Odoi has been appointed National Auditor. The whole party administration will be carefully co-ordinated and streamlined under my personal supervision.

I want to take this opportunity to warn the public against these negative slogans of " one man one car," one man one house." It does no good to anyone, and particularly to those who shout them. I call upon every member of the public to help check these slogans, which do the country no credit.

The Convention People's Party is tested and well-seasoned. It has grown through the years and gathered an invaluable wealth of experience. This experience has strengthened the party and enable it to give leadership to our people and our nation.

The enormous strength the party has gained through the growth of our membership (which is 1,760,000 paid up), makes it important for all of us to exercise extra vigilance to ensure that this strength shall be put to uses beneficial to the country. The tremendous power also exercised by the party through the government which, as I have often repeated, is the agent of the party, must be guarded and used in the supreme interest of the Ghanaian people.

You will see, therefore, that it is exceedingly important from time to time, to examine and re-examine ourselves both collectively as a national party and individually as members. I recently set in motion this self-examination and self-criticism. The response has been remarkable, and I hope this exercise will bring moral health to all of us, and reinvigorate us for higher purposes.

The party's responsibility has doubled. In the pre-independence era, it fought on a single front and concentrated all its effort on the attainment of independence. Now it is engaged on fighting on two fronts. The Convention People's Party is actively engaged in the fight for the total liberation and unity of Africa, and it is also engaged at home in the battle for food, shelter and clothing for the people. This is not an easy task. Many splendid armies in history have been known to go to pieces for trying to fight on two fronts at once. The Convention People's Party, however, is a different type of army. It is the people's own political army, built by their sweat and labour and selected through its battles with imperialism and colonialism so that this double fight can hold no terrors for us. We are determined to conquer and we shall conquer on both fronts. But first we must sacrifice everything for the victory and that means extra hard work for every member of our party. Instructions have been issued and all necessary arrangements made for the membership integration of the various wing organisations of the party. All trade union members who hold Trades Union Congress cards should hand in these cards to the branch party secretary, who will give party membership cards in exchange for the union cards. Those trade unionists who hold both party and Trades Union Congress cards, have been instructed to surrender their Trades Union Congress cards to their union secretaries. Members of the United Ghana Farmers Council have all obtained their party membership cards. Members of the co-operative societies will act in the manner as I have outlined for the Trades Union Congress. Members of the National Council of Ghana Women have never had any card of their own.

The central committee has decided that as from to-day, regional commissioners will become the regional secretaries of the party in their respective regions. The present regional secretaries of the party, of the Trades Union Congress, of the United Ghana Farmers Council, of the National Co-operative Council and of the National Council of Ghana Women, will all be re-designated assistant regional secretaries of the party. Henceforth all appointments to these offices will be made by the central committee.

In each region the party regional offices will house all the integral organisations in one building. In the meanwhile, regional secretaries—that is, the regional commissioners—will hold joint staff meetings periodically to ensure co-ordination of activities of party functionaries in the regions.

We must all of us tackle vigorously and with selfless devotion, the industrial and technological reconstruction of Ghana, and the total liberation and unity of Africa.

But our determination must be based on the realities of our position. As a revolutionary party, we must be prepared, if need be, to adopt revolutionary methods and rid ourselves of anything that will impede our progress.

The Convention People's Party has distinguished itself in this great struggle for the redemption of Africa and no one can think of Ghana without acknowledging the greatness of our party. Indeed, throughout the whole of Africa, the mention of the Convention People's Party brings inspiration, hope and encouragement. Comrades, we have reached a stage where we must take stock and look back. This party, formed on the 12th of June, 1949—that is, eleven years ago—started from small and difficult beginnings. The material resources available to us then were practically nil. There was colonialism and imperialism sitting on our necks and yielding no quarter.

The Convention People's Party carried on and gained not only experience but also strength until, slowly but surely, this party has attained proportions baffling to our foes and detractors and has grown beyond recognition.

This growth has brought with it a great responsibility—the responsibility to give correct guidance to our people and nation and to enable them to have a new world outlook which will create for them new opportunities to rebuild their self-respect, restore their faith and re-discover for themselves their human dignity.

To-day, the party does not stand at any crossroads. It stands at the beginning of a straight road, a straight road to socialism, to a society in which the free development of each is the condition for the free development of all.

In recent speeches I have made clear the position of the party and the government in relation to industries to be owned and operated by the state, and I have also stated our policy in connection with co-operatives. To-day I want to add a word about individual enterprise.

There is nothing to prevent the individual Ghanaian, if his public obligations so allow, from setting up a new business, provided that that business is not in the state sector, and provided that it fits into the pattern of our co-operative and state enterprises. In addition, I want to emphasise that foreign enterprises will still be able to conduct their business in accordance with my earlier speeches. They have never been permitted to operate in the state sector of the economy, and I am confident that, where necessary, they could adjust their operations to fit into our future development of state co-operative or state enterprises.

To travel this road, every member of the Convention People's Party, every Ghanaian man and woman, every boy and girl, all of us together, must work and give service to the nation to the best of our ability. Even the disabled, the blind and the crippled, must be equipped in this great crusade to contribute their quota to the total national effort.

In this respect and with regard to the compulsory free primary and middle school education which is to start next September, I have given instructions that all unemployed persons who are interested in teaching should register in the nearest district education office for employment in the teaching service.

Emergency training centres will be established to instruct these volunteers in teaching methods and appropriate certificates of recognition will be given at the end of the training. To meet the problem of accommodation in schools, I have instructed that the shift system should be adopted. The first shift could be from 7.30 a. m. to 11.30 a. m and the second shift from 12.30 p. m. to 5.30 p. m. This will ensure that no pupil will be left out in the implementation of the free and compulsory primary education scheme.

One of the most important aims of our economic and industrial reconstruction is to increase productivity and efficiency in work so that we can produce more goods at less cost while also improving the quality of the goods and services. To facilitate this, it is my intention to introduce a system of incentives in the form of bonuses, awards and other forms of recognition for meritorious service.

There are some people who wrongly think that party membership confers privileges for selfish ends. There are some also who make the mistake of demanding reward from the party for services rendered. Membership of the Convention People's Party does not confer any such privileges on individuals. Rather, it confers duties and rights on its members.

The duties of a party member are as follows:-

(1) To protect the solidarity and unity of the party at all times.

(2) To pay dues regularly.

(3) To protect the good name of the party under all circumstances and to correct wrong views held against the party

(4) To carry out party decisions and directives to the best of his ability and to ensure that any disregard of such decisions or directives is promptly reported to the appropriate party authority.

(5) To be the first to obey the laws of the country passed by the government.

(6) To defend any action of the party or the government.

(7) To try to understand all party government matters and to explain the same to the people.

(8) To set an example by working hard, efficiently and honestly and by showing a keen sense of responsibility and duty.

(9) To pursue a study of the principles of African socialism and to endeavour to be guided in action by these principles.

(10) To guard jealously any secrets of the party and to maintain constant vigilance in this respect.

(11) To criticise and accept criticism in good faith and spirit and to make frequent self-examination for correction, remembering that all criticism and correction should be made not to destroy but to build.

(12) To be faithful and loyal to the party always and to eschew all qualities of opportunism, nepotism, ostentation, vanity and self-seeking.

(13) To remember that the party is supreme and to do everything within his power to uphold this supremacy.

The rights of members are as follows :-

(1) To take part in all party activities.

(2) To attend meetings and freely express views on all matters in discussion, and to vote according to conviction.

(3) To elect and be elected to party bodies.

(4) To be present in person whenever decisions are taken regarding his activities or conduct.

(5) To address any question or statement to any party body including the national executive and the central committee.

(6) To appeal against any adverse decision against him from his branch party upwards to the central committee, and to the leader of the party in person.

(7) To appeal as a last resort to the national delegates' conference.

If we look at the progress of our nation since independence, we are tempted to sit back and rest, to have a deep sigh of relief, pat ourselves on the back and say we have done very well indeed. This attitude of complacency constitutes a real danger. It is true that we have built roads, expanded education and health services, consolidated our independence, improved agriculture and increased the cocoa yield and made good strides all round. But this is not enough. We have only accomplished but little of the total task ahead of us. The party's role as the vanguard must be exemplary in the discharge of this duty.

The Convention People's Party cannot rest on its oars. Let a spirit of patriotic, fiery enthusiasm grip it once again. It has to lead Ghana to produce great scientists, great technologist, great technicians, great farmers and fishermen, great singers and writers and great administrators.

We must turn out our experts and specialists by the thousands and produce in great numbers the dare-devil go-getters who will produce results, whether they fly an aeroplane thousands of feet above, or mine gold deep down in the bowels of the earth.

I have directed that primary and middle education will be free as from September. This is a great step we are taking to kill illiteracy in the nation. The effects of this will be that, within the next ten years, every Ghanaian man and woman of a certain age will be able to read and write.

Another step I have taken is the compulsory study of science in all schools. The future belongs to the nation that takes to scientific and technological studies and development. Ghana must force the pace of our growth in science and make Ghanaians science-minded. We must produce Ghanaian scientists and technologist to help in the rapid development of Ghana.

Our students will be compelled to study science. Their interest in science subjects must be aroused and sustained. The necessary facilities and incentives for the encouragement of scientific studies and pursuits in our schools will be provided. We are a nation in need and our needs must guide our action. In all these matters, the Convention People's Party must give leadership and I expect that party boys and girls in all the secondary schools and the party study groups all over the country, will take up the challenge and lead the way.

When people quote my statement that our independence is meaningless unless linked up with the total liberation of Africa, I wonder whether they pause to think in concrete terms the effect of Ghana's independence. When in 1957 we achieved independence, only seven African states existed. Within four years of Ghana's independence, and within three years of the Accra Conference of Independent African States and the All-African People's Conference, Africa wears a new look; she has changed the composition of the United Nations and the face of the world.

It is my view that the unity of Africa could be more easily and effectively forged were we to have, throughout the various territories in Africa, a common party with identical aims and programme. This is something we have to think about.

At the moment our efforts are feeble because we are divided and the colonialist and imperialists are taking advantage of this state of affairs to sow seeds of dissension among us. They are doing everything to make it very difficult for us to come together as one people. They know that their interests are finished once Africans come together and realise that we are one people with one destiny. It is for us ourselves to recognise this situation and to fight vigorously against the machinations of these exploiters and to prevent them from teleguiding us and pulling us around on strings like marionettes.

If we were united, France would not dare to flout African opinion with regard to atomic tests in the Sahara.

Our party is a great asset to Ghana. We should keep our eyes and ears wide open and be ever alert to the issues confronting Ghana and Africa. It is important, therefore, that the party should stand together even more solidly than in the past.

All members of the Convention People's Party must make it a point to attend their branch or ward meetings. This year, we have abolished floating membership and every member must belong to a branch. This is to enable proper records to be kept of all comrades, their activities, their contributions and sacrifices for the party—indeed, their complete record.

It is for this reason that no membership cards to individuals are issued from headquarters. All party members, no matter their rank, must obtain their cards from their branches or wards. Arrangements are being made for me to receive my card from my own branch at Nima.

The Convention People's Party will now see to it that all persons who claim membership possess membership cards. Persons who claim to be members of the party but who hold no party membership cards, will be strictly excluded from all party meetings. Everyone of you must therefore obtain your card, if you have not done so already.

In connection with this subject, I wish to stress once more that the cost of the party membership card is 5s. I repeat—5s. No branch or ward has right to sell these cards at a higher price than the authorised cost of 5s. The cards are not priced differently—the same price holds for old as well as new members. The unauthorised practice whereby new members are requested to pay a specific sum of money to the branch coffers before admission is forbidden and must stop forthwith.

Any cases of contravention of this instruction should be reported to national headquarters or to regional headquarters, as the case may be, for the offenders to be dealt with immediately. Anybody who sells a party card for more than 5s. is a *DSULO*. Nobody should be allowed to take advantage of the renewal of membership cards to fill their pockets at the expense of the party.

It is necessary now to turn to the women's section of the party. With the formation of National Council of Ghana Women, that used to be called the women's section which has ceased to exist. The National Council of Ghana Women is an integral part of the party. The National Council of Ghana Women will organise all women in the party and the country, and prepare them especially for the great social task involved in the economic and industrial reconstruction of Ghana. In this national exercise, women will and must play an important part, In the factories and the shops, on farms and in the universities, in the departments and ministries, in all aspects of our national life and at all levels of party activity, the Ghanaian woman must make her presence felt. The National Council of Ghana Women must give a great opportunity to all women to serve their party and country and to make a useful contribution to the total African struggle.

I must now also say something about the party youth league. In the same way, with the formation of the Ghana Youth Authority and the Ghana Youth Pioneers, the party youth league has also ceased to exist. Its functions have been taken over by the Youth Pioneers.

The Ghana Youth Pioneers, having been constituted as the sole youth authority in Ghana, has the responsibility for ensuring that all organisations of youth are conducted in accordance with our national directives and not in relation to any foreign concepts. The youth of Ghana must cultivate great pride and love for our nation and for our African brotherhood.

Comrades, it is glorious and a great honour to belong to the membership of the Convention People's Party, but it is equally a great responsibility. It is we who set an example to the rest in the qualities of honesty, integrity, sense of duty, selfless service and sacrifice. We must guard against the great temptations that accompany power and we must remind ourselves all the time that it is the masses of the people who matter.

Our contact with the masses must remain constant and unbroken and so must our sympathy for them remain deep and unaffected. It is a heavy task, but it is the price of leadership and we, like all other leaders, must pay for it.

Comrades, in our advance to our objective many obstacles may arise. Great difficulties will raise themselves in our way. We must always remember that no difficulties are insuperable.

It is here that the study groups come in. The members of the party study groups must study our constitution, our nationalist objectives and our African relations. They will, of course, learn our socialist principles and apply them as a guide to action.

It is necessary to point out to members of the party study groups, that these groups are not independent units of the party. Every student of a party study group must be a member of his branch or ward.

Officials of the party who conduct these groups, must ensure that those comrades who attend study group meetings equally attend their branch meetings. Attendance at party study group meetings cannot be a substitute for attendance at ward or branch party meetings. These meetings of the party study groups are open to all party members. In fact, a student of a party study group has a greater duty to attend branch or ward meetings. Conductors of party study groups must bring this home to their students.

I come now to party officials—the men and women paid by the party to carry out administration of the party's affairs.

Party administration, since April, 1960, has greatly improved.

In the first place, before that date, office accommodation was so small that the national secretariat was unable to function in its fullest expression. In April last year, however, we opened this magnificent building as the national secretariat of our party, and set up a modern administrative machinery, fully equipped for the proper discharge of its responsibilities. This act constituted a great advance in our party administration.

The party secretariat has since functioned with efficiency and precision and party matters now receive the proper administrative attention they deserve.

Party officials must always be aware of their heavy responsibility. They are paid by the party to give service to the party, but their role is more than that of paid servants. They must throw their body and soul into their work and, being party members themselves, they should realise that their whole time must be at the disposal of the Convention People's Party. They must live exemplary lives and, like Caesar's wife, must be above suspicion.

Party officials, whether at national headquarters or at regional headquarters, must know that it is a great honour and privilege to work for the party as a recognised party official and they should show gratitude for this opportunity to serve.

Some party officials, instead of realising this position, drag themselves low and misuse their party position in many undesirable ways. Any party official caught in any such act will be dealt with in most ruthless manner. Party officials should exercise patience in their dealings with the masses and show sympathy when other comrades approach them for direction, guidance and help.

They have a difficult task, but I am sure that, with confidence in themselves and faith in the party, they can carry out their duties with conviction and efficiency.

Discipline is important in any organisation. Discipline is that which sustains the solidarity of the party and I urge all party members to bear this in mind in all their activities.

Comrades, I charge you to keep our flag flying high. We have won several victories. We shall win yet more victories for we have faith in our cause and confidence in our party and hope for the future.

I salute you. Freedom!

13

POLITICS ARE NOT FOR SOLDIERS

TO CADETS OF THE GHANA MILITARY ACADEMY

May 18, 1961

I am happy to be with you today. I have been greatly impressed by all that I have seen, and I am particularly encouraged by the progress that has been achieved so far in this academy. For my part, I find these visits most useful, providing as they do the welcome opportunity to get to know you individually. I only wish that my duties would permit me to come here more often to watch you in your training.

I must congratulate you on your very smart turn out on parade. This is a clear indication of your great determination to uphold the prestige of the army to which you belong. I know that you all look forward to the day when, at the end of your training, you will be commissioned as officers of the Ghana Army. I must warn you however that apart from the real opportunity that this will afford you, it will also bring you face to face with great responsibilities. You must appreciate that to be an officer in the army is not going to be easy. The highest qualities of character and standards of ability will be demanded of you. The qualities expected of an officer are that he must be a gentleman; his integrity must be beyond doubt; he must be completely honest and loyal in all his ways, and remain above suspicion of any kind.

In your role as soldiers, your physical courage will be taken for granted; but as officers it is not sufficient merely to have physical courage. You must have moral courage as well, the courage that will prompt you to speak the truth at all times whatever the cost, and to shoulder your responsibilities however burdensome they may be.

As officers, you must have a high sense of social idealism and dedication not only to the armed services to which you belong, but to your government and to your country. Consideration for yourselves must never be allowed to stand between you and your duty. You must at all times have confidence in your superior officers in the army, in your Commander-in-Chief, and in the political leaders in the government. You must have confidence that the government is doing what is best for the country and support it without question or criticism. It is not the duty of a soldier to criticise or endeavour to interfere in any way with the political affairs of the country; he must leave that to the politicians, whose business it is. The government expects you, under all circumstances, to serve it and the people of Ghana loyally.

A good officer must be strong not only physically, but mentally. This mental toughness will enable you to endure, if need be, not only great mental strain, but physical discomfort. I must stress again that the quality of selflessness is absolutely vital to a good officer. Your loyalty must be unquestioned. As an officer of the Ghana Army, your loyalty is to your government and your country on the one hand, and to your men and those whom you serve on the other. If ever there is any conflict, it is your self-interest which must be sacrificed.

I wish you success in your training at this academy and the best of luck for the future.

TRAGEDY IN ANGOLA

The National Assembly
May 30, 1961

Mr. Speaker, Member of the National Assembly,

I am taking the opportunity, before the National Assembly adjourns, to address you on the situation which now exists in the Portuguese colonies of Africa and, in particular, in Angola.

This situation has taken a serious turn and is threatening the peace of Africa, and because of this what is now taking place in the Portuguese colonies is the concern of all African peoples and, indeed, the concern of all peace-loving peoples of the world. It is essential we do our utmost to rouse world opinion. Indiscriminate slaughter of men, women and children is at this very moment taking place in Angola. Forests are being set on fire by incendiary bombs dropped from Portuguese aircraft, thus burning alive thousands upon thousands of men. women and children for no crime other than being African. Armed Portuguese settlers roam the towns and countryside killing and looting at will. Such is the dreadful picture of events in Angola painted in the world press of to-day. No newspaper has estimated the African dead at less than 20, 000. Some put it as high as 100, 000. In such circumstances there must be revolution and the revolt in Angola has already broken out and is making headway.

The facts told in column after column in the newspapers of the world make one thing clear. The issue of Angola is a question of African nationalism and of human liberty and decency. It is in no sense an ideological question. Here no issue of communism versus capitalism arises. The question is reduced to the most simple formula. Which countries have sufficient interest in humanity to step in and stop the slaughter in Angola?

The irony of the whole situation is that while the great powers, like Britain and France, are adjusting their thinking and actions to the requirements of modern times and have recognised the principles of self-determination for their colonies, Portugal sticks stubbornly to the idea of a "Portuguese soul," "Portuguese" territory and a "civilising mission" in a mediaeval fashion and seek to perpetuate these under a most degrading, humiliating and oppressive rule. The attempt to cover this up by talk about Euro-Africa is nonsense, geographically and geopolitically. The avalanche of nationalist fervour which is rolling over Africa and toppling imperialist and colonialist governments has touched Angola, and touched it in a substantial manner.

In Angola, inspite of the enervating force of slave labour, in spite of the absence of any form of proper education, in spite of all the grinding disabilities and misery suffered by the people there, that country has now entered the African nationalist revolution and it will never be the same again. However, if the Angolan people are left to fight their battle entirely on their own, their sufferings and casualties will be enormous.

The evils of Portuguese colonialism are realised by all African states without exception. We should therefore be able to go united to the assistance of the people of Angola and it is most important that the differences of approach which we have on other problems should not prevent our mobilising the full strength of African opinion against what is taking place to-day in those parts of Africa controlled by Portugal.

A genuine desire for unity is not enough. We must understand the forces which bring about such a tragedy as is happening in Angola to-day and which in its final solution must spur us on to African unity —the only force that can prevent the recurrence of a similar tragedy. I stated before the United Nations, and have stated many times elsewhere, that what is happening in the Congo can be repeated in other African territories under colonial a rule unless the Africans themselves unite to save Africa from the misery of these tragedies.

It is impossible to examine the question of the Portuguese colonies in Africa unless they are looked at within the frame-work of the Africa situation as a whole.

Superficially, the Portuguese colonies represent the old colonialism in its most classic form. In fact, however, they are also an example of neo-colonialism in its latest and most dangerous guise.

We shall not therefore be able to deal with the problem of the Portuguese colonies—and, indeed, the colonial question itself—unless we understand and are able to detect and meet the dangers and calamities of neo-colonialism. For it is the neo-colonialism, hidden in the background, rather than the front of classic colonialism, which makes the issue in Angola or the Congo so difficult to resolve.

First, to be frank, the colonial power, Portugal, is herself a sort of colony. Indeed Portugal is an interesting example of early neo-colonialism of the early nineteenth century.

Once the owner of a powerful empire, Portugal had by the beginning of the nineteenth century become entirely dependent upon other powers. In the economic and financial sphere Portugal had become a client state of the United Kingdom. Militarily she depended upon Spain. The dominant role of the United Kingdom can be illustrated by the numerous occasions when the United Kingdom expressed itself willing to give away the Portuguese colonies in Africa, generally to appease Germany. This colonial attitude of the United Kingdom towards Portugal leads subconsciously among certain sections in the United Kingdom to a defence of the Portuguese position under any circumstances. Thus the United Kingdom feels obliged not to support any resolution at the United Nations which criticises Portugal in any way. The British Foreign Secretary's speech in Lisbon last week, in which he said that Portuguese policy in Africa, like that of Britain, was based on respect for human personality, is another example of the same trend. Such a remark made in the face of the known facts of the Portuguese atrocities in Angola can only be attributed to a kind of congenital blindness suffered by the United Kingdom so far as Portugal is concerned.

However that may be, the Ghana Government is bound to have the impression that the statements made in Lisbon by the British Foreign Secretary, and the promise of the dispatch of British troops to Portugal at this time, whatever the purpose of such a speech or visit, give assistance to Portuguese colonialism.

The fact that Portugal can master such a degree of support cannot however be attributed solely, or indeed mainly, to her ties with the United Kingdom.

In the neo-colonial world of Southern Africa, the Portuguese colonies and all that they stand for are essential for the purpose of depressing African wages, preventing trade union organisation and maintaining high profits for expatriate-owned industries and farms.

Let me give you just one example of how Portuguese forced labour is essential for the neo-colonial economy of neighbouring states and territories.

In 1959, last year when there are available statistics, only one-third of the labour force of nearly half a million workers employed in the South African mines came from South Africa. This figure has only been obtained painfully and laboriously by the pass laws and other methods of pressure which can now be applied within South Africa.

At the beginning of the century, in the early days of South African mining and before pass laws and the policy of repression of Africans generally had really got under way, it was impossible to recruit in South Africa free labour to work in the mines. The Portuguese colony of Mozambique was used, therefore, as a source of forced labour and in 1903, for example provided no less than 89 per cent of the total labour force of South African mines. This supply of conscript labour is still an economic necessity to South Africa if wages are to be kept down and trade unions prohibited.

Accordingly, the South African Government has entered into an actual treaty with the Portuguese Government to supply labour for the mines.

This barter deal in human beings, known as the Mozambique Convention, is divided into three parts, The first part fixes the maximum and minimum numbers of Africans who are to be recruited and provides for the payment to the Portuguese Government of registration, engagement and monthly fees in regard to each recruit obtained. Part 2 of the convention gives to Portugal certain advantages in regard to railway traffic and rates, and part 3 provides for customs advantages in return for the supply of cheap labour. The basis of the agreement is that in return for an undertaking by the Portuguese Government that the South African Chamber of Mines shall be the sole recruiting agency in Mozambique for mines labour, the South African Government formally undertakes that 47.5 per cent of the sea-borne import traffic to the mining areas of South Africa shall go through the Portuguese harbour of Laurenco Marques. Originally, the maximum figure for labour recruits under the convention was 90,000 a year. In 1940, however, the Portuguese Government agreed to raise the total to 100,000 a year in return for an agreement by the South African Government to export 340,000 cases of citrus fruit each year through Laurenco Marques.

The mines where this Portuguese contract labour works may be situated in South Africa or in the Federation of Rhodesia and Nyasaland, but the shareholders of the mines are as likely as not to be resident in the United States, in the Unite Kingdom, in France or Belgium.

There are therefore powerful influences in these and in other countries who are determined to use their political influence to ensure that their countries support Portugal in maintaining its forced labour system and all the tragedies that flow from it.

What happens in regard to labour for the mines so far as South Africa is concerned is merely, of course, an example. The existence of the Portuguese colonies make cheap labour possible not only in South Africa but in all the neighbouring colonial territories, and is an important element in the profits not only of mining but of many other industries, including plantation farming.

All those with a financial interest in such enterprises cannot therefore allow Portugal to lose her colonial possessions.

Perhaps less important, but of considerable influence in securing further support for Portugal among certain circles abroad, is the fact that much of the investment in the Portuguese colonies is not Portuguese at all, but international.

The Benquela railway, running from Benquela, with a 20-mile addition along the Atlantic coast to Libito, to Beira in Mozambique on the Indian Ocean, stretches for 1,700 miles. It was built largely by British interests to bring out ores from the mines of Kantanga. Traversing the great Angola plateau, it passes to a point above Elisabethville in Congo, and then links up with the Rhodesian railway system, after which it passes on to Beira. Ninety per cent of the stock of the Benquela railway is held by the British holding company of Tangayika Concessions, domiciled since 1952 in South Rhodesia.

Tangayika Concessions is linked up with the copper interests of North Rhodesia and with Union Miniere and other industrial concerns in the Congo. Through interlocking directories, this company is linked with Forminiere and certain diamond interests which, together with De Beers, the great South African mining company, control the Angola diamond Company with mines in the Luanda province.

This company is a state within a state. It possesses a prospecting monopoly over five-sixths of Angola and a labour conscription monopoly over most of the Luanda province, one-third the size of Ghana. One half of its profit goes to the state, the other half to the private shareholders.

No wonder it can influence policy whichever way it likes and holds in its hands the lives of the Africans of the Luanda province.

No wonder it maintains the fiction that a permit to visit its mines must come from Lisbon.

For these economic reasons, Portugal can count on heavy backing from vested financial interests throughout the world. Her position in maintaining her colonial dictatorship is, in addition, immensely strengthened by her membership of the North Atlantic Treaty Organisation.

Let me at this stage state the policy of the Government of Ghana in regard to such organisations as NATO.

We do not object to—indeed, we have no right whatsoever to object to—other states forming defensive alliances. In so far as such alliances contribute towards peace they are indeed to be encouraged and, in any event, the steps which other nations takes to preserve their own security are entirely a matter for the judgement of the independent states concerned. Ghana is in favour of an African High Command, which would provide for the defence of the African continent, and it would be illogical for a country which supports such a proposal to criticise other countries who have formed defence plans on a continental basis. Nevertheless, I consider that Ghana is completely justified in opposing any military alliance in so far as that alliance is directed towards the maintenance of colonialism and imperialism in Africa.

The criticism which Ghana has at the moment of the North Atlantic Treaty Organisation has nothing whatever to do with its defensive aspects. Our complaint is that certain members of the organisation appear to use their position in it to obtain arms and financial support for the worst type of colonial oppression and suppression.

One must ask the question: Why is Portugal in NATO at all? Portugal is an impoverished country without military forces of any value and the only possible strategic argument why it is necessary to include her in the NATO alliance is that she possesses some bases of doubtful value in the Azores.

Do the NATO powers really consider that the possession of these bases is worth the goodwill of the African continent?

Portugal is only able to wage a colonial war because fundamentally she has the backing of the North Atlantic Treaty Organisation. If this backing were withdrawn tomorrow and Portugal was excluded from NATO, Portugal's colonial rule would collapse the day after. Is it not worth the while of the NATO powers to secure the end of an intolerable regime in Africa through the sacrifice of the most doubtful military advantages which they obtain through their association with Portugal?

We must, however, accept the realities of the present situation.

Portugal is a member of the North Atlantic Treaty Organisation and there are the strongest financial and economic pressures being exercised to maintain Portuguese colonialism.

The African states can only assist the people of Angola, therefore, if the African states themselves escape from the influence of NATO, or of any other defence alliance, and of neo-colonialism. I believe that if African freedom and unity is to be achieved, it will be by a policy of positive neutralism and non-alignment and by the rejection of all neo-colonialism.

At the moment, neo-colonialism is establishing itself among a number of African states.

Take for instance the European Common Market, which is but the economic and financial arm of neo-colonialism and the bastion of European economic imperialism in Africa. The treaty of Rome, which brought into being the European Common Market, can be compared to the treaty that emanated from the Congress of Berlin in the nineteenth century.

The former treaty established the undisputed sway of colonialism in Africa; the latter marks the advent of neo-colonialism in Africa.

In another sense, it may be said that the Treaty of Rome, particularly in its effects on Africa, bears unquestionably the marks of French neo-colonialism. Indeed, the former French Investment Fund for Economic and Social Development which has become the Fund for Financial Assistance and Co-operation and the European Fund claiming to help newly independent African states economically and financially, are one and the same thing.

The Fund for Economic and Social Development in its implementation in the colonial territory simply reduces that territory to the position of an exclusive market for the economy of the metropolitan country.

If we want to achieve unity in Africa, then at this moment of African nationalist revolution we cannot rely on international organisations that have their concepts and their loyalties beyond Africa. We must create our own organisations and, when we do so, we must adhere loyally and rigidly to them. Creating our own African international trade union organisation, we cannot individually opt to associate with other international unions, for this will do exactly what we must be on our guard against. It will divide our loyalties, it will weaken our own organisation. The African national trade union organisations can affiliate only with the All-African Trade Union Federation if we are going to maintain our identity and our strength. When we are all joined within the All-African Trade Union Federation, then we can associate as a single apex body with the other international apex bodies, for then we shall be equal and not weaker parties to be used by the stronger

I have discussed this question of neo-colonialism at some length because it is highly relevant to the unity of action among African states which is essential to secure effective action in regard to Angola

What I have said explains, I hope, the main difference which Ghana has with the Monrovia powers. Nevertheless, this difference should not lead us into a slanging match between individual African states. I much deplore the press attacks which have been made from all sides as a result of what is in effect a genuine difference of opinion, springing from the grave difficulties of having to solve, within a very short space of time, the many problems which we have inherited from a colonial regime.

I would like to see a truce in press warfare between African states, and I suggest that we might inaugurate this truce by declaring a unilateral "cease fire" in Ghana. What the present situation requires is not abuse, but argument. If we are to convert others to our point of view, we shall not achieve this by calling them names. We may achieve it, and I believe that we shall, if we can secure a forum where the issue we put forward can be impartially examined.

Let me now come in detail to the situation in the Portuguese territories and particularly in Angola.

The first essential which we must make the world realise is that the Portuguese territories in Africa are slave states and have always been slave states.

Outright slavery, called by that name, continued in Angola until some one hundred years ago. Though theoretically abolished in 1875, slavery was still continued by various methods which were put into definite legal shape by a Portuguese law of 1899. This law, which is still in force to-day provides that "all natives," that is to say all Africans, are subject to "a moral and legal obligation" to acquire by labour the means of subsisting or " bettering their social condition." Under this law every African male in Angola, which is in practice interpreted as those above the apparent age of ten years, is obliged to show either that he has worked for six months in the year previous to investigation or that he is working at the time of the investigation. Since the investigators are those who are charged with recruiting the labour, it is unlikely that they come to any very objective decision on this matter. What in fact happens is that employers who want forced labour indent for it to the Governor-General. The Governor-General then allocates forced labour in accordance with a theoretical calculation of the numbers which may be available. Request are then sent to the local administrators up and down the country until they reach what would be the equivalent of a district commissioner in old colonial times in Ghana. The district commissioner then proceeds to enter into a contract for the services of the forced labour. The contract is, however, not signed by the workers concerned; it is a contract entered into collectively on their behalf of by the chiefs and headmen who are entrusted with the duty of producing, within the times given, the specified number of labourers who are required.

It is true that less than half of the labour employed in Angola is officially classified by the Portuguese authorities as contract labour, that is to say, forced labour. Over half of it is theoretically voluntary labour but in practice the position of the voluntary labourer is not better than that of the forced labourer. The voluntary labourer cannot leave his job because if he does he will become liable to be classed as "idle " and therefore subject to forced labour. His only chance of escape is by emigrating from the Portuguese territories and attempting to obtain work in other neighbouring states. Portuguese sources have estimated in the ten years previous to 1947 that over one million people had left the Portuguese colonies by way of clandestine immigration. Indeed the only way to evade the torture of life in the Portuguese colonies is to escape across the border. But not all the people can go, and those who are left behind often bear the brunt for those who have gone. And they have no avenue of articulation, no medium through which they can make their grief known, their sorrows heard, nowhere to turn for mitigation of their plight. When others have been in the same position, there have been those who have raised their voices for them. All over the world we have heard cries for people who are reputed to exist in conditions which would be paradise to the African of the Portuguese colonial territories.

In an attempt to cover up this system of slavery, the forced workers are, in theory, paid wages. In fact, however, three quarters of these wages are deferred until the end of their contract period and are not handed over until the state has deducted taxation. This is so high that at the end of their period of employment, they are left with scarcely any balance at all.

For example, in one authenticated case, a man employed in the fishing industry had, after he had worked for four years, a final balance of £3 2s. 6d

The indescribable misery of Angolan conditions has continuously been brought to the notice of the Portuguese Government, but nothing except paper reforms have been carried out. In 1947 Captain Henrique Galvao, Deputy for Angola in the Portuguese National Assembly and Senior Inspector of Overseas Territories, investigated these conditions on the request of the Portuguese Government and submitted a comprehensive report.

Galvao had been appointed because the Portuguese Government expected from him, as a fervent government supporter, a whitewash report which they could use in the United Nations and elsewhere. Infact, Captain Galvao was so shocked by what he saw in Angola that he changed his political views and submitted an honest and balanced account of what was taking place in the Portuguese possessions overseas.

As might be imagined, the Portuguese Government did everything possible to suppress the report and Captain Galvao was thrown into prison for his presumption in telling the truth. Ultimately he escaped from Portugal to appear dramatically on the scene when he led a band of seventy brave men to seize the Portuguese liner *Santa Maria*.

One of Captain Galvao's chief criticisms of the Portuguese regime was its deceit. In theory and on paper it had abolished forced labour on behalf of private firms and individuals. In fact, forced labour was being stepped up.

He described how in Angola, openly and deliberately, the state acts as a recruiting and distributing agent for Labour on behalf of a band of settlers who as though it were quite natural, write to the Department of Native Affairs for "a supply of workers." The word "supply" is used indifferently of goods or men. He had no doubt in his mind as to the existence of slavery but he explained—and I quote his actual words—"in some ways the situation is worse than simple slavery. Under slavery, after all, the native is bought as an animal; his owner prefers him to remain as fit as a horse or an ox. Here the native is not bought, he is hired from the state, although he is called a free man. And his employer cares little if he sickens or dies, once he is working, because when he sickens or dies his employer will simply ask for another."

These opinions he backs up with horrifying statistics showing in some cases a death rate of 40 per cent among the forced labourers.

Forced labour of this sort can of course only be maintained by the exercise of the utmost brutality both on the part of the colonial authorities and the employers themselves. The situation has recently been made much worse by the introduction of a large settlers class.

The precarious state of the Portuguese economy at home makes it necessary for Portugal to export its own poverty and to compensate citizens for the work which the state cannot provide them with at home by dispossessing the African population of the colonies and by providing, for incoming Portuguese, land and cheap African labour. Just as the farmers of South Africa are much harsher and crueller employers than are the mines and the big industrial concerns, so are the Portuguese settlers, in the main, more ruthless and cruel than the international big businesses which have been established in Angola.

One final consideration explains the Portuguese ferocious

attempts to put down the present liberation movement and their determination at all costs to maintain their hold upon their African colonies.

Twenty three per cent of the total export trade of Portugal goes to her African possessions where she can maintain a system of excluding other competitors. Textiles, which are the largest single import into the Portuguese territories, are 89 per cent Portuguese. The second largest import is wine. It all comes from Portugal. In the same way as the early European trades in West Africa dealt largely in gin, so Portugal finds in its colonies one of its finest outlets for its alcohol.

The real question is whether, if these exports from Portugal were to be cut off, the Portuguese economy could survive.

Portugal is at home an old fashioned despotic oligarchy, established and maintained in the interest of a minute group of extremely wealthy families, and at the same time is the poorest of all European countries. There is therefore a potentially revolutionary situation in Portugal itself. All those who are afraid of social change in Europe thus become the allies of Portuguese colonialism since its maintenance appears to be the only method by which Portugal itself can be saved from revolution.

All the injustice, social degradation and slavery of the Portuguese regime has now reached a climax in the revolt in Angola. In such a situation, what practical and immediate steps can we take?

The independent African states should band themselves together to end once and for all Portuguese and other colonialism in the African continent.

Thanks to the initiative of the Afro-Asian group at the United Nations, the Security Council will next week debate the Angola question. All pressure should be put on the United Nations to see that a positive and effective resolution is adopted. Actions through the United Nations is of the greatest importance and Ghana will support to the full any positive proposals which may be made by the Security Council. Our experience, however, of United Nations action in the Congo should warn us against trusting exclusively to action by the Security Council for resolving the crisis in Angola.

Resolutions of the Security Council require to be backed by action by all African states, working in concert and within the framework of the United Nations Charter.

I have already sent a message to the heads of government of each of the independent African states calling their attention to the serious situation in Angola.

What more can we do?

Our immediate task is the enlightenment of the conscience of mankind. We must build a machine in co-operation with all other independent African states to expose in detail exactly what is taking place in Angola to-day. We must appeal by every peaceful means at our command to the people of Portugal itself, to put an end to this unjust and inhuman colonial war.

We must make concerted arrangements for the assistance of the wounded and the refugees from Portuguese territory. We must appeal to the great international trade union movements of the world for concerted action against Portugal. We must appeal to dockers not to load arms destined for Portugal. We must appeal to seamen not to carry goods of any description to or from Angola.

We must use African external broadcasting systems to publicise throughout Africa, and beyond, the facts about what is happening in Angola to-day.

But, as I have said before, and as I emphasised in closing my address to you, above all we must seek unity of action among the states of Africa on this issue, irrespective of our differences in other matters.

Divided we can do nothing for the people of Angola and the Revolutionary Front for the Independence of Angola unite and go forward together in their grim fight to achieve self-determination and freedom for the people of Angola.

The African's duty is clear. All Africans must stand united behind them.

If all this should fail, then we will have to find some other means.

Mr. Speaker, Members of the National Assembly, I now leave you to your deliberations.

15
NEW HORIZONS

SESSIONAL REPORT ON THE FIRST SESSION OF THE FIRST PARLIAMENT OF THE REPUBLIC OF GHANA

MR. SPEAKER AND MEMBER OF THE NATIONAL ASSEMBLY,

In accordance with Article 25 of the Constitution I send you this Message and Report on the First Session of the First Parliament of the Republic of Ghana.

The desire of the people of Ghana to reach new horizons of equality, economic sufficiency and respect among the nations of the world was consummated in the establishment of the Republic on the first of July last year. The celebrations marking our entry into new era and the culmination of our political struggle were attended by representatives if no less than 46 foreign countries.

Since Republic Day, in keeping with our open door policy of peace and friendship with all nations, we have been privileged to welcome five distinguished heads of state in the persons of Emperor Haile Sellassie of Ethiopia, President Leopold Senghor of Senegal, President L. I. Bershney of the Union of Soviet Socialist Republics, President Tito of Yugoslavia and President Yameogo of Upper Volta.

We have also had the pleasure of welcoming Prince Moulay Hassan (now King Hassan II) of Morocco, and Mr. Julius Nyerere, the Chief Minister of Tanganyika.

In pursuit of the challenging ideal of African unity and closer collaboration in Africa, Ghana decided in the Conakry Declaration of December to establish a union of African states together with the Republics of Guinea and Mali. Practical methods of strengthening this union have been formulated and the first quarterly meeting of the heads of the member states was held in Accra in May.

The Casablanca Conference held in January was followed in February by a meeting in Accra of the Foreign Ministers of the Casablanca powers and later by a meeting of officials of the Casablanca powers. These meetings have set the peace for the movement for unity and collaboration in the entire continent of Africa. They have helped Ghana to bring into focus political and social injustices in South Africa, Southwest Africa, Angola, Portuguese East Africa, Algeria and Congo.

By far the most important international problem which has exercised the government during the session has been the Congo crisis. During the session I paid two visits to the United Nations and made a personal appeal for a solution to the Congo problem on the lines of the eight-point resolution supported by the Casablanca powers. I am glad to say that many of the recommendations contained in this resolution have already been adopted by the United Nations.

In the belief that the newer powers of the world have a definite role to play in the promotion of international peace, we have continued to help the efforts of the United Nations towards easing world tension. The recent Cairo conference of non-aligned powers was a step in this direction.

Mr. Speaker, I wish now to turn to domestic affairs. On the 20th of February a government White Paper setting out the details of the Volta River Project was presented to the National Assembly. The National Assembly thereupon approved the proposals for the financing of the scheme and authorised negotiations to proceed in accordance with the terms set out in the master agreement.

In subsequent negotiations the terms and conditions of the loans, the conditions under which power would be made available to the consortium of North American aluminium companies, the lease of a site for the establishment of a smelter at Tema, and the entire fiscal arrangements under which VALCO would establish and operate a smelter at Tema have been agreed in principle and the necessary legal instruments are now being prepared.

You will recall that tenders for the main construction works for the dam, saddle dam, power house and appurtenances were opened on the 16th of February, and on the 12th of May I announced that the contract had been awarded to an Italian consortium known as Impresit-Girola-Lodigiani and E. Rechi.

The contract for the Akosombo dam construction having been awarded, the arrangements for the loans financing and for the construction of the smelter having been agreed in principle, and the Volta River Authority having been established by an Act of Parliament, we have come to the end of the first stage in the implementation of this gigantic project. Thus has been fulfiled the promise made to the people in the 1951 election manifesto of the Convention People's Party. It is my hope that when completed, the Volta River Project will stand as a moment to posterity—evidence of the profound dedication of my government and party to a better life for the people.

Steady progress has been made in the programme for the diversification of our economy.

Among the major decisions taken during the session was one to increase the capitalisation of the Ghana Aluminium Company by which the investments in the company are to be increased from £G125,000 to £G1,000,000.

A preliminary agreement has been reached for the establishment of a cement industry with a capital investment of £G4,000,000.

A soap factory has been established at Tema with a capital of about £G2,000,000.

An agreement has been signed with the Italian petroleum company AGIP—to establish a petroleum refinery at Tema at an estimated cost of £G8 1/2 million. It will be capable of producing 1.2 million metric tons of refined petroleum products a year.

The government has set up a state mining company to foster the expansion of the mining industry. The corporation has taken over five mines from private companies and the Ankobra power station has also been acquired.

Since July, 1960, over 20,000 persons have been employed by employment centres which were set up under the Labour Registration Act of 1960. The demand for employment services has become so great that 20 additional employment centres are being established.

A National Apprenticeship Board has been established to undertake the effective organisation of vocational and technical training within industry. This will promote the rapid training of skilled artisans and craftsmen for the generation development of the country.

To relieve wage earners of the burden of the cost of living the minimum wage was fixed at 6s. per day for the whole country. A general increase of 1s. per day was awarded to all wage earners whose income did not exceed £G610 a year.

Co-operation activity has extended into many fields. Out of 640 registered societies over 100 were registered during the session. The new ones included societies such as agricultural producers' co-operatives, distillers' co-operatives, livestock breeder's and local crafts co-operatives. Expansion in co-operative activity has also been undertaken in the fishing industry and poultry farming.

During the session the Builders Brigade has been reorganised. Two senior police officers have been seconded to the brigade as national organiser and deputy national organiser respectively. Brigade senior officers have been trained at the Military Academy and in the Police College, The brigade has made good progress in the field of agriculture. Several acres of land have been cultivated for food, tobacco and rubber. The brigade has also rendered other services such as clearing sites, building barracks and constructing sidewalks and parks.

Remarkable progress has been made in the production of economic crops other than cocoa. The quality and quantity of coffee produced in the Volta Region has improved with the establishment of processing facilities. The development of the rubber industry in the Western Region has been resumed with great vigour. The increase in tobacco growing in the Volta Region has been phenomenal.

In the interest of the farmers it has been decided that as from the mid-crop season this year the United Ghana Farmers Council should be the sole buying agent for the Cocoa Marketing Board. Suitable arrangements have been made to enable the farmer to sell his produce to the marketing society in his own area in order to rid himself of the middleman.

From September next primary and middle education will be free and compulsory. Plans are well in hand for implementing this new scheme.

Improved salary scales for the teaching service were introduced in July and a new grade of principal teacher was established.

The establishment of the Ghana Young Pioneers was a milestone in the programme of youth training and in our efforts to inculcate in the youth of the country a sense of service to God and state, patriotism, honesty and human dignity.

A library to be devoted to African affairs is nearing completion. It will be known as the Padmore Research Library, in memory of the late George Padmore.

With the establishment of the Central Organisation of Sports in July, public interest in sports has stimulated throughout the country. Last year Ghana competed in the Olympic Games for the first time. She took part in the Rome Games and achieved the honour of being the only West African country to win a medal.

Work on the central prison at Nsawam has been completed and the prison began to be used in October. Satisfactory progress has been made on extensions to existing prisons. Trade training facilities in the prisons and at the Borstal Institution have been expanded.

A scheme has been started under which hospitals will be modernised. Under construction are modern operating theatres at six hospitals, seven dental clinics, nurses training schools and hostels in six towns and eighteen health centres.

During the session 107 doctors, 24 of whom are specialists, have been recruited. To provide for the staffing of hospitals 32 medical and four dental scholarships have been awarded for the training of Ghanaians overseas. Twelve Ghanaian doctors have been sent overseas to take specialist courses.

In furtherance of our policy of co-operation and collaboration with the newly independent states of Africa, the Division of Public Construction has embarked upon an ambitious programme of road construction to link Ghana with the states lying to the north, west and east of our frontiers.

Considerable progress has been made in the supply of pipe-borne water, and the provision of dams in the Northern and Volta Regions has been satisfactory.

A firm of Greek consultants has submitted a preliminary report on the planning of the Accra-Tema-Akosombo area, and with the appointment of a special development commissioner for Accra the pace of development in Accra has already begun to quicken.

In February the government acquired complete control of Ghana Airways by taking over from British Overseas Airways Corporation (and Associated Companies) Limited, their interest in the corporation. By the conclusion of international air service agreements Ghana is now connected by air to all independent African states. The airline's fleet has been improved with the addition of modern inter-continental turbo-prop and pure jet airlines from the United States, the Soviet Union and the United Kingdom. Full ownership of the Black Star Line was acquired by the government when the shares held by the Zim Israeli Navigation Company were bought over. Three of the eight ships under construction in Holland have been launched and the first of them, the Pra River, recently arrived in Ghana on her maiden voyage.

Work on the construction of Tema harbour has continued satisfactorily. A restricted operation of the harbour commenced in July.

In the field of international trade we have maintained our adherence to the general agreement on tariffs and trade and the principles of multilateral trade and most-favoured-nation treatment. However, in line with our policy on non-alignment and also in order to diversify both our sources of supply and our export markets, we have concluded general trade agreements on a most-favoured-nation basis with Czechoslovakia, Yugoslavia, and the Soviet Union.

We have been in close contact with Guinea, Mali, the Niger,

Upper Volta and Dahomey in an effort to achieve an economic union in West Africa.

During the session a salutary effect on trade was caused by the transfer of the Cocoa Marketing Company from London to Accra, the sale of all diamonds won in Ghana through the Accra Diamond Market and setting up of the Timber Marketing Board.

Firm action by the government against organised gangs of criminals whose activities might have threatened the security of the state has resulted in a marked reduction in the incidence of crimes of violence. In all other respects the internal security of the state has been maintained.

Africanisation in the army has proceeded steadily. During the session, fifty-four Ghanaians were commissioned into the armed services.

A contingent has been maintained in the Congo and it has earned high praise for its general efficiency and the valuable service given under the United Nations command.

The survey and re-planning of a naval base at Sekondi was put in hand early in 1961.

An operational flying station has been constructed for the Air Force at Takoradi.

A publicity secretariat has been established under my personal supervision.

The external broadcasting installation at Tema has been completed. Through it the "Voice of Africa" will be heard throughout the world.

The subscription fee for radio rediffusion has been reduced from 7s. 6d to 5s. a month.

Plans are under examination for the assembly in Ghana of battery radio receiving sets.

The Ghana Film Unit has become a film corporation, and arrangements have been made to turn the Ghana News Agency into the All-African News Agency.

In order to enable local government bodies to play a more effective part in the development programme of the central government, plans have been completed for the establishment of larger councils, viable and self-sufficient in all respects.

The government has decided to establish two universities—the University of Accra and the University of Science and Technology at Kumasi. A university college is also to be established at Cape Coast. Interim councils for the universities have been appointed.

Three important research units have been established. They are the National Institute of Health and Medical Research, the Forest Products Research Unit and the Road Research Unit.

Members of the National Assembly, I wish to thank you for the funds which you have voted for the public services during this session.

16
THE CPP 12TH ANNIVERSARY
June 12, 1961

Today is the 12th anniversary of our great party and it is an anniversary with a difference. This anniversary meets the party and the nation with me as general secretary of the party and President of the Republic.

This fact constitutes a remarkably historical landmark for our people, for it shows that, as I have often said, the party and the nation are one and the same, namely: the Convention People's Party is Ghana and Ghana is the Convention People's Party.

Comrades, it is needless for me to ask you, therefore, to recognise this outstanding fact: that a very grave responsibility lies on the shoulders of us all, not only as Ghanaians, but also as members of the Convention People's Party which, no matter what may be said by our detractor, remains right in the front of the struggle for the total liberation of Africa and the union of the independent African states.

If you cast your eyes across the continent and look to South Africa, Congo, Angola, South West Africa, Kenya, Central Africa and the other areas of our continent where colonialism still flourished, you will agree with me that our task is only just beginning. We have a duty to gird our loins, strongly, to order our lives austerely, and to clench our teeth grimly, in order to enter the battlements of the enemy and smash them to pieces. This we must do at all cost, with African nationalism as the liberating sword.

In the areas where physical colonialism has been smashed, colonialism in its new subtle forms has reared its head. This new colonialism is even more dangerous, because it operates unseen; but it operates all the same most effectively, twisting independent countries around its ugly fingers by the manipulation of economic gadgets and the profession of benevolent friendship which is as hollow as an empty shell.

Comrades, the Convention People's Party, which has weathered so much storm and which is a veteran in this field of combat, must stand by Africa day and night. We must stand in the supreme interest of our motherland and fight against these evils of imperialism, colonialism and neo-colonialism, and set an example of sacrifice, determination and courage.

We have already given ample evidence of our capacity for government and have debunked the threadbare accusation that Africans lacks the ability to rule themselves. We have shown friendship to all and sundry and have made it quite clear that we do not move East or West but only forward, which means pro Africa; but we have adhered strictly to our policy of positive neutralism and non-alignment and whatever we have done, we have always placed Africa first.

Comrades, we are intensely interested in the preservation of peace in the world, for Africa has a vested interest in peace. But we have made it abundantly clear and will not budge an inch from the position that we are unalterably opposed to all forms of imperialism, colonialism and neo-colonialism and not even the great sacrifice of life could shift us from this ground.

So on this 12th anniversary of our party, it is of the most absolute importance that we should all rededicate ourselves to this enormous task and remember constantly that Africa can only be saved by Africans.

The Convention People's Party, must keep a keen eye on the attempts by the imperialists and colonialists to balkanise Africa. It must fight ruthlessly and relentlessly to break down all the artificial barriers which have been erected in the crisis-cross dissection not only of the land surface of Africa but also of the material life of our people, separating father from son, brother from sister, mother from daughter with the inhuman purpose merely of extracting the wealth of Africa for the benefit of the people of other lands. We cannot—we must not—allow these barriers to remain.

The trails of the future shall be even more perilous than those we have survived in the past. But inspired by the rugged and austere experience gained by the lean years of our political revolution, the Convention People's Party must move forward to these new challenges fortified by the conviction that our cause is just and that an organised and disciplined party like ours can never stand still.

Finally, that Convention People's Party must mobilise our total man-power for the industrial, economic, technological and scientific reconstruction of Ghana, so that we can produce the necessary conditions which shall mean an abundance of every good thing for our people and the greatest welfare for the masses.

Long live the Convention People's Party.

Long live Ghana.

There is victory for the cause of Africa.

PADMORE THE MISSIONARY

THE OPENING OF THE GEORGE PADMORE MEMORIAL LIBRARY

Accra
June 30, 1961

We have met here today to do honour to the memory of George Padmore, by dedication to him this building and this library. The library has been built in order that the great ideals of Pan Africanism and the noble cause for which George Padmore worked and died may be continued. It is altogether fitting and proper that we should take this action at this particular time. Today, more than ever, we are called upon to come to grips with the challenge of our time as we enter a decisive phase in the struggle for the total liberation and unity of the African continent. Whilst the struggle for the independence and unity of Africa continues, we are made increasingly aware of the appearance of a new colonialism, the ugliest and vicious form that has yet reared its head, namely, an economic and military colonialism. As we begin to see before us the gradual unfolding and realisation of the independence and unity of our African continent, our thoughts turn naturally to George Padmore who in his innermost being was by any reckoning, one of the greatest architects of the African liberation movement.

This library will be known as the "George Padmore Memorial Library."

Comrade Padmore's life was spent in the development of African nationalism. His fertile brain was full of ideas which he assidiuously mobilised, through his writings and lectures, for the African cause and in the supreme service of humanity.

Burning with missionary zeal, comrade Padmore unflinchingly dedicated himself to the exciting task of African liberation and

African unity. I do not intend, on this occasion, to relate at length how I first came in contact with George Padmore, or to speak of my subsequent personal relationship with him, I have borne testimony to this elsewhere. Suffice it to say that there is not one of us who had the privilege of working with Padmore and sharing his rich mind of thoughts who cannot say with Mark Anthony: "He was my friend, faithful and just to me." To me personally Padmore was more than this. He was a pearl of priceless value, a real and deep-loving elder brother. His loyalty to me was pure, unquestioned and convincing. It was not based on emotionalism: it was a genuine spiritual and intellectual loyalty. He was loyal to me because he believed implicitly that what I stand for is the only thing that can lead to the total emancipation of the African continent, and as a West Indian he also felt that the emancipation of Africa would have its repercussions on every person of African descent throughout the world. No matter what hour of the day or night I called upon him, he was there at my side, ready to help me. So often he expressed concern over me: "Take care of yourself," he would say. "We need you." Little did I think that he would leave me alone so soon. Shortly before he died in London he told friends that the believed I would have to bear the brunt of African freedom fight whether I like it or not.

George Padmore had many sterling qualities. He was a worthy patriot, a powerful orator, a skilled politician, able philosopher, journalist and author. He was above all, a great freedom fighter.

As a patriot, Padmore served his race with unparalleled distinction. As a politician he sought to break the myth of white supremacy and inspired Africa nationalism which today has become a militant force in the destruction of imperialism and colonialism. As an orator he was impeccable and unflustered. No degree of heckling could drive him off his point which he always held tenaciously and with consummate courage. As a scholar, he had a broad view of world affairs; as a philosopher, he was not trammelled by his own experiences, but drew extensively and intensively on the experiences of others. His philosophic exposition of Pan Africanism shows his profound depth of thought and rich quality of mind. As a journalist, he was a prolific writer and a nightmare to the colonialists and imperialists. His trenchant but factual articles exposing the cruel machinations against colonial peoples frequently brought him into bitter conflict with the colonialists and imperialists who loathe and despise the truth. As an author, his impact on the literary world is profound and his works can be found in the homes of every African nationalist, Conscious of the fact that the price of freedom is eternal vigilance, George diligently and passionately dedicate his whole life to the noble struggle for African liberation.`

Comrades, ladies and gentlemen, I feel there could be no more fitting and lasting honour to such an illustrious patriot than the monument such as the one we are about to dedicate to the memory of our beloved comrade.

There is indeed an urgent need for a centre of research into the life of the people of the African continent to which the student can turn for current information and historical narratives in this period of tremendous change and political upheaval. No one appreciated this need for libraries and research better than George Padmore. He was one of the most widely read and most prolific authors on African affairs in this day, and this library, which will bear his name, will provide the raw material of scholarship on the whole of Africa. I am confident that by co-operation with other centres of African studies, this library will play a great part in the increasingly important task of making available publications from all parts of the world on the current African scene. Books, pamphlets and periodical articles will be indexed and classified so that the enquirer can have immediate access to the latest information, irrespective of language.

I hope that the George Padmore Memorial Library will eventually issue selected bibliographies on matters of current interest in Africa. There is widespread misunderstanding and ignorance about the newly-developing independent nations of Africa. We are often misrepresented either because our critics do not take the trouble to check the facts or because they rely upon outdated and biased information.

"The speed of change, both social and political, in modern Africa is a challenge to those who attempt to interpret its meaning through the printed and spoken word. A research library on African affairs can provide a focal point for African studies where facts, statistic and reliable comment can be readily obtained.

This building is a notable addition to the service of the Ghana Library Board. It is yet another example of how modern materials can be adapted to tropical conditions, with functional arrangement and equipment to meet the most exacting requirements of scholars and research workers, Here will be housed the tools of research that distinguish all great libraries— books, periodicals, government documents, reports, abstracts and indexes, together with the most modern devices for the preservation and storage of knowledge—microfilm and photocopying equipment. Air-conditioned storage has been provided in the basement for large numbers of document and bound periodicals, thus freeing the shelves of the main library for the most current and up-to-date material likely to interest the user. I consider that this building makes a significant contribution to library planning.

A good national library is at once the repository of a nation's culture and wisdom and an intellectual stimulant. In this library, there shall be no national frontiers: for here shall be stored the cumulative experience, the collective wisdom and knowledge about the entire continent of Africa and the assessment, revaluation and studies of observers from all over the world. Here is an important addition to the specialised services of a future national library in Ghana. Under the agency of the Ghana Library Board will be carried out the tasks of selection, indexing and preservation which underlie the whole process of building up a specialised library collection. National bibliographical and documentation services have not yet received serious consideration in Ghana. An annual publication listing all books and government reports published in this country, as well as books written about Ghana from other countries would be an invaluable service, and the foundation of the George Padmore Memorial Library should make this possible. We can look forward to the time when a unified bibliography of Africa outlining the progress and achievements of the African peoples will be made available

At this point, comrades, I would like to emphasise the desirability of developing in our society the power of intelligent reading; the progress and prosperity of our society will be largely determined by the quality of our knowledge.

And here, I wish particularly to call upon the youth and workers of the nation who have hitherto become victims of passive amusements and purposeless hobbies to desist from unprofitable activities which clog their aspirations and sap their energies to take up reading as their hobby and to make the fullest possible use of this library.

"Reading maketh a full man," says Francis Bacon. No one can deny that purposeful reading as a leisure-time activity, apart from helping the development of individual personality by enlarging his conception of man and matter and promoting his general efficiency by broadening his outlook, gives to the tired mind what rest and sleep give to the tired body.

Let this library therefore be a shrine of wisdom and patriotism for all African students in this country and elsewhere. May it be an instrument of scholarship for the study of the African peoples and an inspiration for those who work towards African freedom and unity.

And now, friends, comrades, ladies and gentlemen, I have great pleasure in declaring the George Padmore Memorial Library open.

18

WORK FOR GHANA AND THE FUTURE

BROADCAST TO THE NATION
September 20, 1961

I had hoped that on my return to Ghana after a prolonged visit to the USSR, China and countries of Eastern Europe, I would be able to give you a detailed account of my mission and discuss with you the lessons which we could usefully learn. Many of the countries I visited have made spectacular progress in their economic and cultural development. I am convinced that we have much to learn from them on how to speed up our industrialisation and our educational progress and how to improve our economic planning, Ghana must develop her own social and political institutions best suited to her circumstances, and the personality and temperament if her people.

However, I must leave to a future occasion a full discussion of these matters and of the ideas and schemes I have in mind for the progress of our people and country.

Tonight I wish to talk to you about the stoppage of work which started in my absence and which continues to disturb the normal economic life of the Sekondi/Takoradi community.

Let me discuss with you the procedures which the strikers have adopted and the reasons which they have given for their surprising behaviour. This is not an ordinary industrial strike arising from a dispute between employers and their workers on conditions of work. Its ostensible object is to force the Government and Parliament to withdraw legislation initiated by the Government and approved by Parliament concerning the entire economic and financial policy and programme of work of the Government. These strikers have taken it upon themselves to determine what the Government's policy should be, not by constitutional means, but by resorting to an illegal strike. No government in this world would allow itself to be coerced by the illegal actions of a very small section of community. If the railway workers of Takoradi disagree with the policies of their constitutionally elected Government they have every right to make their views known to the Government, through their Members of Parliament whom they chose at the last elections, or, if they prefer, through the Trade Union Congress, which is the spokesman for the organised workers of the nation.

But what is the nature of these supposed grievances which have prompted these workers to take this illegal and disgraceful action?

They object to the compulsory savings scheme, to the monthly deduction of income tax and to the Government's taxation policy as a whole, in fact to the whole budget. This budget, which I outlined in my speech on the 4th of July, was arrived at after the most careful consideration by the Cabinet of the services which the Government must provide for the well-being of its people and of the fairest and most equitable way of finding the money to pay for these services. As I emphasised in my speech, since independence we have been able to provide public services on a scale far greater than were provided during the whole period of colonial rule, both of the kind which yield an immediate benefit to everybody, such as public health, education, roads, etc., and also those which serve to develop the nation and strengthen its security and independence. At the same time, the cost of these services has been greatly increased by the Government's action last year to improve the standard of living by increasing wages.

Nobody can deny that we have made spectacular progress as a result of the expanded activities and efforts of the Government. For a time it was possible to pay for those expanded services without increasing the burden of taxation because the world cocoa price made it possible for us to earn the money through our exports. Everybody knows that the economy of Ghana greatly depends on the world price of cocoa—a factor over which we have no control. When the price of cocoa fell last year it became clear that the Government's services and its development expenditure could not be paid for without higher taxation, unless the money was found by a large reduction in the price of cocoa paid to farmers. I was firmly convinced that if the situation called for additional sacrifices, these must be distributed among all sectors of the community and not thrown on the farming community alone, as has substantially been the case all these years. The Government has therefore decided to meet the problem in the most honest and equitable way, partly by the cutting expenditure as mush as it was possible and partly by raising additional taxes on commodities and incomes.

The bulk of the increased income taxation will fall on the companies. There has been no substantial increase in personal income tax but a new system of collection has been devised to ensure that all shall pay what is due from them. Finally we proposed that internal development expenditure should be met by all sectors of the community being asked to contribute to National Development Bonds. This is a compulsory but patriotic scheme which is not taxation.

As I announced in my speech, the purchasers of State bonds are being asked to lend money at interest to the Government, which will be repaid in full, for the development of the country. In this way the benefit of economic development will accrue not only to the community generally but also to those individuals who contribute, in proportion to their contributions. You help yourselves by helping the nation, by saving for your own future.

Nobody has to my knowledge come forward with any suggestions of a better way of raising the money for development. We could have cut expenditure by much more in preference to imposing new taxes. But if we had done this we would have had to dismiss public employees and workers on a substantial scale and thereby caused far more hardship than the new taxes and contributions could possibly cause—quite apart from the ill effects which reduction in the standard of public services would have had on the life of the whole nation.

The strikers of Takoradi say they object to the compulsory savings scheme, which requires them to save only 5 per cent of their incomes—I repeat, only 5 per cent of their incomes—to help their country. People earning less than £G10 a month are altogether exempted from this contribution. They say they object also to paying a very modest income tax which is only payable on incomes on excess of £G40 a month.

Obviously there must be some sinister motive in this matter. The majority of the people who are now on strike because they want a withdrawal of the budget provisions are altogether exempted from the compulsory savings scheme, and from paying income tax, and are not directly affected by them. What, then, is their grievance? Even those who have been asked to make the 5 per cent compulsory contribution and who are liable to pay income tax, which in no case can amount to more than a very small fraction of their income, forget that only last year the workers in the lower income brackets got a wage increase of 22 per cent.

When I arrived back in this country in 1947, workers were receiving wages as low as 9d. a day for their labour. As a result of the direct agitation and action of the Convention People's Party under my leadership, workers were receiving a minimum pay of 4s. a day in the rural areas and 4s.6d. in the municipal areas at independence. To-day, again as a result of my interest in the workers, workers receive a minimum pay of 6s. 6d. a day throughout the country. Surely there is more to this Sekondi/Takoradi strike than meets the eye.

I have tried to explain to you tonight how the budget is made up of two parts, first, a programme of work and services and, second, the means by which that programme is to be paid for. The taxation—direct and indirect—and other contributions which the people have been called upon to pay are needed to enable your Government to continue the work it has set out to do. That programme consists of many things, for example, the bringing of more and better medical and health services for you and your children. For this alone we shall require over ten and a half million pounds this year as compared with three million in 1957. In 1957 there were scarcely 100 Government doctors in the whole country. To-day there are about 250 Government doctors in employment and another 300 under training and during this year we hope to increase the number of practising Government doctors to about 350. For education, on which the future depends, we shall this year, be spending over fifteen million pounds, as compared with nine million in 1957. In 1957 there were 570,000 children at primary and middle schools. This year the enrolment is 762,000, an increase of nearly 200,000 in four years.

The secondary school enrolment in 1957 was 9,800. This year it is expected to be 16,500 or almost double the 1957 figure. These are some of the things for which we need money and also some of the things which we will have to forgo if we cannot raise money. I have not even touched on the expenditure for our new elaborate housing programme. Nor have I touched on the expenditure for defence, which we must maintain in order to ensure the security of our independence and sovereignty.

It was with great sorrow and shame that I learned that some of the leaders of the strikes in Sekondi/Takoradi had addressed telegrams to foreign organisations seeking their support. These people have declared openly that they are determined to force the Government to alter its entire fiscal policies by unconstitutional means. In this action they have shamelessly and openly sought foreign support. Is more evidence needed that we must be constantly on the alert if we are to maintain our hard-won independence?

There is something even more sinister than this. In an unsigned paper circulated through the country and purporting to come from the strikers, it has been suggested that our Republican Constitution should be abolished and that we should go back to the system of having a Governor-General, and thus revert to a past which we have just discarded. This clearly exposes the purpose of this strike and those who hide behind the strikers and instigate them.

We, the people of Ghana, have played our part in breaking the shackles of colonialism in Africa. In the few short years since independence there have been great achievements which we can look on with pride. This things could not have been done except by a singleminded people immovable in their faith and strong in their unity. These qualities have already changed the course of history: we are creating an Africa fit for heroes to live in. It is unpardonable to indulge in action which will endanger these achievements and give our detractor cause for hope that we cannot live up to the bright promise of the 6th March, 1957.

There is last word I have to say. It was you, the people of Ghana, who chose me as your leader. I accepted this high position in a spirit of humility and dedication—humility, because I am conscious that the leader of a people emerging from colonial domination has a hard, exacting task; dedication, because it is only in a sincere spirit of dedicated service that a leader can be worthy of his people.

I stand by these ideas to-day as I did at the beginning of our struggle.

I must emphasise, however, that so long as I remain your President, I shall not tolerate any subversive and lawless acts aimed at upsetting the Constitution and endangering the security and safety of the State.

Tomorrow is a public holiday—Founder's Day. The entire nation recognises that I am the founder of the new State of Ghana. This holiday is not only in my honour, but also it is an occasion to remember the foundation of our nation and all that went before, and to re-dedicate ourselves to the cause of our nation. Let us therefore, as from tomorrow, resolve that we will forget our selfish interests in the greater interests of the nation and the future.

I ask all of you who have still absented yourselves from work to resume work by 7. 30 a. m. on Friday, the 22nd September. Those who do not do so will have given clear indication that they and the instigators behind them are determined to bring about the overthrow of the Constitution by illegal means.

Good night and good luck to you all!

19

THE VOICE OF AFRICA

THE OPENING OF THE GHANA EXTERNAL BROADCASTING SERVICE

October 27, 1961

Ladies and Gentlemen,

I am happy to be with you this afternoon. I consider this occasion to be of great significance to Ghana and to Africa as a whole. We are gathered here to inaugurate the External Service of the Ghana Broadcasting System, a service which we hope will be a powerful force in our struggle for the liberation and unity of the African continent.

Although the ceremonial opening of our External Broadcasting System takes place this afternoon, the service itself has been in operation on a trial basis since the middle of June this year. From that day programmes have been broadcast for three hours daily from our Accra studios in English, French, Hausa, Swahili and Arabic. It is hoped to add programmes in Portuguese soon. Altogether, this station transmits each day twenty-one news bulletins from our studios in Accra. In addition, news talks and newsreel are broadcast every day to all countries on the African continent and throughout the world. It is our hope that in the not too distant future we will expand this service to cover as many as fifteen languages.

The news is presented from an African standpoint and covers events in all Africa and the world. From this station we shall broadcast all-African news bulletins presented without concealment or distortion. Our compatriots in Africa and our friends now have the opportunity of hearing each day, in the language they understand, accurate and factual accounts of day-to-day events which may not be available to them from foreign-controlled and foreign-dominated radio stations operating in and broadcasting to their countries.

From this station also, commentaries and news talks will be broadcast every day, giving Ghana's standpoint in international and African political affairs.

These programmes must reflect all that is best in the everyday life of our people. They must project the development that is taking place in Ghana and Africa generally, presenting the true image of Ghanaian and African life and culture, and setting it in an international context. We will thus be able to demonstrate not only the contribution that Ghana and the other countries of Africa have to make to world civilisation and to the peace and welfare of mankind, but also that our continent is capable of a political union.

Through this service, therefore, we shall step up the effects which we are already making to show that ours is a progressive and vigorous country, ready to make her contribution to the peace of the world and the progress of mankind.

To our African compatriots and freedom fighters, to our brotherly independent states of our continent, our message is: For too long have we been subjected to vile and vicious propaganda designed to cast doubts on the ability of the African to manage his own affairs. Even when we became independent, the whole apparatus of colonialism was turned on us in an effort to disunite and separate us. There are no signs that the flood of this malicious propaganda is diminishing. On the contrary, it has been increasing: but the greater the pressure and attack, the stronger and firmer is our stand of non-alignment and neutralism. This means that the voice which will go out will be truly African—African in content, outlook and imagination.

It will speak in clear unequivocal tones in defence of our rights. But it will be directed against no one except those who wish to trample upon our freedom and who desire to reduce us to a position of subservience, political and economic dependence, always working for their own interest and caring little about our own African humanity. We stand for peace and friendship with the world, We are neither anti-West nor anti-East. We have our own way of life, a socialist way based on a sound cultural foundation and an African background. Those who wish to understand our actions must first begin to study and appreciate this background, They should not judge us from ignorance and they should not expect us to become mere copy-types of their past or present, however good these may be to themselves.

In this External Broadcasting System we now have a voice which will boom and resound across the shores and over the mountains and valleys, carrying with it a message of hope and encouragement to our compatriots in our beloved continent. The voice of this service will not necessarily be the Voice of Ghana; indeed, it will be the Voice of Africa.

From this station will go out a force and power based on goodwill, which will generate a new confidence in the African, especially those of them who are not yet free from the shackles of colonialism and imperialism. From this station, symbol of the true Voice of Africa, we shall continue to fight for our complete emancipation, assisting in the struggle for the total liberation of the African continent, and the political unification of the African states. This voice will rise in a steady crescendo, and it will never fail or falter on the cause of peace, friendship and understanding between men and the nations of the world.

We are confident that the service which we are formally inaugurating today will be a powerful force, sustaining the assault that we have launched against the ramparts of colonialism and imperialism in all their forms and manifestations.

Your Excellencies, Mantsemei, Nananom, Ladies and Gentlemen:

I now have the greatest pleasure in declaring this building and this service open and in commissioning it to the service of Ghana and Africa and, indeed, to the whole world.

20
FLOWER OF LEARNING (1)

AT HIS INSTALLATION AS FIRST CHANCELLOR OF THE UNIVERSITY OF GHANA, DURING THE INAUGURATION OF THE UNIVERSITY

November 25, 1961

CHAIRMAN OF THE UNIVERSITY COUNCIL, YOUR EXCELLENCIES, LADIES AND GENTLEMEN:

It is a great honour for me to accept office as Chancellor of the University of Ghana. The ceremony which we have witnessed in this Great Hall this morning has been most moving and impressive. I realise and appreciate the heavy responsibilities which fall on the interim Vice Chancellor of the university, the professors and all those who from now on will be associated with the university. As your first Chancellor, I shall do everything in my power to assist in promoting the successful development and prosperity of this university.

Higher institutions of learning in Africa were in the past designed to suit the colonial order and their products therefore reflected the values and ideals of the colonial powers. Consequently, colonial institutions of higher learning, however good-intentioned, were unable to assess the needs and aspirations of the societies for which they were instituted. We have on numerous occasions denounced these institutions as ivory towers, lacking the necessary sympathy with the people, walking in the clouds with their feet dangling in the air. The University Commission to which I have referred, interpreted the tasks of the university as follows:

They should be "responsive to the sense of urgency that exists in a developing nation; to use its resources imaginatively and effectively to contribute to the economy of the social organisation; to interpret their studies for the benefit of the people and to learn from their problems."

I am not in any way belittling the academic foundation that has been laid here over the last thirteen years. We are grateful to the men and women whose work and sacrifices have made this university possible. We are grateful to them and shall ever remember their contributions to higher education in Ghana.

We have never had any doubt, however, about the intellectual capacity of the African. History tells us of the great medieval civilisations of Africa and the part that higher institutions of learning played in the academic and cultural life of the African. Centres of learning such as Walata, Djenna and Timbuktu had a singular impact on African education in medieval times. There is no doubt that in the University of Sankore, medieval Africa had already qualified to be numbered amongst the foremost intellectually-inspired of the world. If the University of Sankore had not been destroyed; if Professor Amed Baba, author of forty historical works, had not had his works and his university destroyed; if the University of Sankore as it was in 1591 had survived the ravages of foreign invasion; then the academic and cultural history of Africa might have been quite different.

Africa wanted to revive and revitalise its traditions of scholarship and progressive endeavour but, instead, slavery and the slave trade set in and plagued our continent, threatening the very existence of the race.

The story of the development of the African personality during this period is pathetic. Owing to the degradation of slavery, the African was not allowed to develop his peculiar qualities, nor was the African genius allowed full expression. It is estimated that, during the period of slave trade, fifty million Africans were taken away from this continent. But the story of slavery in Africa, stark and dark as it is, is nevertheless partly relieved by the work of a few African intellectuals of the 18th century who, in the face of great odds, convinced Europe that if the normal process of diffusion had been allowed, the course of events in Africa would have been different.

It is interesting to refer at this point to a few of these African intellectuals who, despite slavery, scaled the intellectual heights and achieved eminence and renown.

Attobah Kwodjo Enu, of Ajumako, was bought by an English slave trader and shipped to Grenada, but was later redeemed by Lord Hoth and educated in London. Enu wrote his reflections in English and Latin, condemning the institution of slavery: "Calculated to move the heart of monsters but not those of the slave dealers."

William Ansa Sesraku of Anomabo, also sold in slavery, became an outstanding poet of his day. These lines which he composed in London in 1749 may be of interest to you:

"Whate'er is great and gay around me shine,

And all the splendour of a court is mine,

And knowledge here, by piety refin'd,

Sheds a blest radiance o'er my bright'ning mind

From earth I travel upward to the sky,

I learn to live, to reign, yet more, to die,

I long to tell thee, what, amaz'd, I see,

What habits, buildings, trades and polity!

How art and nature ye to entertain,

To write the wonder here, I strived in vain

Each word would ask a thousand to explain.

The time shall come, O! speed the ling'ring hour!"

Let me mention also the case of Anthony William Amo, who in the first half of the 18th century, at the height of slave trading activities, became a professor in philosophy at the University of Wittenberg and counsellor at the Court of Berlin. He wrote dissertation in Latin and Greek. After thirty years in Europe Amo returned to Ghana and died at Shama.

In our endeavour to organise and promote researches into the African background and history and to assess the full structure of this period, I have asked Mr. William Abraham, a product of this university and a Fellow of All Souls, Oxford, to work on the life, times and philosophy of Anthony William Amo. I could mention also Mensah Sarbah, Attoh Ahuma, Casely Hayford, Phillip Quarcoo, and our own Aggrey. I could continue to speak of Africans capable of repeating the whole of the Koran from memory, Africans versed in Latin, Greek, Hebrew, Arabic and Chaldaic, celebrated Africans who were corresponding members of the Academies of Science of Europe and America.

The desire of learning has always been a marked feature of our life; but it is in the spread of education after the abolition of slavery in the last century that this desire became most evident. The diligent efforts made by the various missionary bodies during the last century in providing formal education were greatly aided by the equally great desire of the chiefs and people to organise communal labour and other resources needed for the purpose. By the middle of the 19th century, however, the intense desire for learning had passed the mark where the "three Rs"—reading, writing and arithmetic—could normally be accepted as the hall-mark of literacy. And here the educational and industrial programme of the Fanti Confideracy of 1871 is significant:

Art. 8 — *That it be the object of the Confederation*

—To make good and substantial roads throughout all the interior districts included in the Confederation.

—To erect school-houses and establish schools for the education of all the children within the Confederation, and to obtain the services of efficient schoolmasters.

—To promote agricultural and industrial pursuits, and to endeavour to introduce such new plants as may hereafter become sources of profitable commerce to the country.

—To develop and facilitate the working of the

mineral and other resources of the country.

We have met here this morning to inaugurate the University of Ghana. Within the next few days, we shall meet again at Kumasi to witness the inauguration of the Kwame Nkrumah University of Science and Technology.

The University College of Ghana was established as a result of the recommendations of the report of the Asquith Commission on Higher Education in the Colonies and those of the report of the Elliot Commission on Higher Education in West Africa. Both reports were published in 1945. The report of the Elliot Commission put forward a minority recommendation that there should be one university, to be sited in Ibadan, for all the then British territories in West Africa, and territorial colleges in Nigeria, Sierra Leone and Ghana, and this minority view was readily accepted by the Colonial Office. The reaction, however, of the people of Ghana who, since the days of Sir Gordon Guggisberg, had been hoping to have a university institution of their own, was swift. After much discussion in the local papers and pressure from the African members of the then Legislative Council, there was a change of heart and the University College of the Gold Coast came to be established as part of the general development of university education on West Africa.

It was the one great desire of the people of Ghana to have their own institution within which men and women were to be brought up in their maturing years in their own traditions and within their natural environment.

This wish was consummated in 1948 when, by an Ordinance, the University College of the Gold Coast was established "for the purpose of providing and promoting university education, learning and research." The University College of the Gold Coast which, after the 6th March, 1957, became the University College of Ghana, was thus established to become the foundation of the University of Ghana which we are inaugurating today.

The year 1948 is a significant one to us in Ghana. It marks the national re-awakening on the path of our political, economic and social struggle to become an independent sovereign state. It was the beginning of the national awareness of the full meaning and content of true freedom and liberty which we enjoy today. It is therefore worthy of note that our struggle for the possession of our own university institution which would be the cornerstone of our educational progress should have been such a happy prelude to the beginning of our final purposeful and most determined struggle for political freedom. The establishment of the University College of Ghana was, therefore, a source of much encouragement and pride to a nation that was determined to support higher education at all costs by the very generous endowment of the farmers of this country and grants from the general revenue of the Government to which the men in the street contributed in no small measure. The establishment of University College of Ghana and its eventual growth have been the natural development flowing from a national desire and pride. The ordinary people of the country provided the soil, the climate and the neccesary nutrients which have facilitated the growth of a university. We are therefore witnessing today an event of the greatest moment of our times the flowering of a national ambition.

The growth of the University College of Ghana into the University of Ghana has been slow and deliberate. There has been no attempt to rush developments merely for the sake of having a university of some sort. For nearly thirteen years the University College of Ghana was in special relationship with the University of London in order to ensure high standards in the academic planning of examinations leading to degrees in the arts and sciences. In other words, adequate care was taken to ensure that the standard of learning and scholarship which the University of Ghana has inherited was acceptable anywhere in the world. In this respect, Ghana is grateful not only to the University of London which, through these difficult, formative years, has readily given advice when approached with particular problems of the new institution of higher learning, but also to other British universities which have in some way been associated with the University of London in this difficult task. By the attainment of university status I trust that both the lecturers and the students of the college have accepted the challenge to maintain the high academic standards already set. It is my fervent hope that the university will be able to maintain all that is good from its associations with other universities and improve upon them. May the University of Ghana develop and prosper in her own natural African environment.

This, ladies and gentlemen, brings me to the place of African studies in this university. But before then, let me re-state the objectives which the international commission, to which I have referred, considers appropriate to the universities of Ghana. These are:-

> *(1) To provide opportunities for education in all those branches of human knowledge which are of value in modern Ghana for the maximum number of Ghanaians who are capable of benefiting therefore.*
>
> *(2) To equip students with an understanding of the contemporary world and, within this framework, of African civilisations, their histories, institutions, and ideas.*
>
> *(3) To undertake research in all fields with which the teaching staff is concerned, but with emphasis where possible on problems—historical, social, economic, scientific, technical, linguistic—which arises out of the needs and experiences of the peoples of Ghana and other African states.*
>
> *(4) To enable students to acquire methods of critical independent thought, while at the same time recognising their responsibility to use their education for the benefit of the peoples of Ghana, Africa and of the world.*
>
> *(5) To provide opportunities for higher education and research for students from other parts of the world, and particularly from other African states.*
>
> *(6) To develop close relationships with the people of Ghana and their organisations and with other universities.*

The development of African studies in this university therefore, is of great importance, value and urgency; once more I quote the Government's White Paper on the recommendations of the commission, in this respect.

"The Government accepts, in principle, the commission's proposal for the establishment of an institute of African studies, to be based upon the University of Ghana but to have some measure of autonomy. The institute will have a most significant role to play both in the university and in the national life, and it should therefore be developed on an imaginative scale. It is a matter of necessity that the building up of the institute will have to depend to a great extent upon scholars from overseas; in this connection the Government will welcome the co-operation of overseas universities releasing teachers and research personnel for temporary attachments to the institute and will be ready to receive assistance from foundations and other bodies, in various parts of the world, which promote social and cultural research. It is the Government's hope, however, that within a few years the institute will have a firm basis of African scholarship and that it will become an internationally recognised centre for the advanced study of African history, language, sociology and culture and of contemporary African institutions."

I am happy to learn that the Institute of African Studies is already committed to these objectives and I appreciate the efforts being made by the institute to give every student here some course in African studies. This is vital if we should eradicate the colonial mentality which our contact with Europe has induced in us and rediscover ourselves with confidence and a distinct world outlook. It is important for every student to maintain his links with the African scene, and thus understand the great cause of African unity to which we are committed. All Africa is moving closer and closer together. Doubtless it will finally find its existence in a union of African states.

In opening the first Conference of Independent African States at Accra in April, 1958, I made the following statements:

"There is a searching after Africa's regeneration—politically, socially and economically—within the milieu of a social system suited to the traditions, history, environment and communal pattern of African society. Notwithstanding the inroads made by Western influences, this still remains to a large degree unchanged.

"In the vast rural areas of Africa, the people hold land in common and work it on the principal of self-help and co-operation. These are the main features still predominating in African society and we cannot do better than bend them to the requirements of a more modern socialistic pattern of society."

This, ladies and gentlemen, is the foundation of pan-Africanism. We expect you who are studying here, with all the facilities at your disposal, to search into the communal basis of our society.

Ladies and gentlemen, let me in conclusion say how anxious I am that as many people as possible who deserve university education should obtain the opportunities for acquiring it. I am convinced that this is one of the surest means of securing individual development and natural progress. No sacrifices should be too great for achieving this. Great changes are taking place in the world to-day, and the frontiers of knowledge are daily expanding. Ghana and Africa must look forward and ahead.

We have centuries of damage to repair, and upon us is placed squarely the responsibility for this great task of recovery. We must discharge this responsibility with speed and success.

In 1957, we told the world that Ghana's independence was meaningless unless it was linked up with the total liberation of the African continent. At that time only eight African states were independent. We called the very first Conference of Independent African States in Accra the following year and this made stronger and more intense the struggle against colonialism and imperialism and, after only four years, the number of independent states has increased to nearly 30.

But this achievement, however impressive, is only the first step towards the political, economic and cultural unity which must come if we are to survive balkanisation and neo-colonialism and eventual political enslavement.

In all your work here one thing must be uppermost in your minds: The freedom and development and unity of Africa and the moral, cultural and scientific contribution of the continent to the total world civilisation and peace.

As you can see from my very brief sketch of the cultural history of this country, for over three centuries we have yearned for the opportunities which we can only now place at the disposal of our students and our generation. This has been made possible because we are now free. The opportunities here are great. The buildings here are some of the best you can find anywhere in the world. The laboratories are first class, the library is good and tuition is free. These are facilities which most of us here longed for in our time. May you all be worthy of this great heritage.

21

STRENGTHENING THE BONDS OF INDUSTRY

OPENING OF THE UNITED STATES EXHIBITION

November 27, 1961

LADIES AND GENTLEMEN,

I am grateful to the United States Ambassador, Mr. Russell, for involving me to open this National Exhibition and Trade Fair which the United States Government has decided to hold in Accra at this time.

In recent years, we have been pleased to welcome many such shows to Ghana. This particular exhibition, however, is unique in that it is the first of its kind to be organised here by the United States Government. As a result of these exhibitions and trade fairs, we have had a good opportunity of seeing for ourselves many aspects of the economic and industrial development of the countries sponsoring them.

Such exhibitions have served to fire our imagination, and to inspire our people in our determination to proceed as rapidly as possible with the economic, industrial and technological reconstruction of our country to which we are committed. It is for this reason that I am happy that yet another exhibition has been arranged by the United States Government.

In my message which has been placed at the entrance to this exhibition alongside a message from President Kennedy, I have expressed the hope that all Ghanaians who come here will find much to interest them, and much to learn. I want to repeat this, and to express the further hope that all who see this exhibition will go away from it more determined than ever to contribute their full share toward Ghana's economic reconstruction.

Ghana and the United States of America have maintained very happy trade relations over the years. The United States is the largest importer of Ghana's cocoa. We, for our part, have for a long time obtained from the United States our principal imports of machinery, transport equipment, fuel and chemicals. These trade relations with this United States are very important to us. I am sure that this exhibition will lead to the opening up of further sources of trade and commerce between the two nations.

True to our policy of positive neutralism and non-alignment, we are against any form of discrimination in economic matters. We believe that capital and technical knowledge have no respect for political frontiers.

We make no apology, therefore, for the steps we have taken recently to strengthen our trade and economic relations with the Soviet Union, Eastern Europe and China. Our main interest is to seek opportunities for the rapid industrialisation and mechanisation of our agriculture and to diversify our economy generally. For we know that it is only if we become economically strong and politically stable that we can carry through with sufficient determination our policy for the freedom and unity of the African continent.

We in Ghana to-day have to face many of the problems which almost two hundred years ago faced the founding fathers of the United States of America.

In the same way as their ideas were ridiculed and misrepresented in the old world, we too have to face a constant barrage of misrepresentation from the foreign press which invents false news about our actions and puts the worst possible construction upon everything we do. I understand full well the reason for this attitude. These articles are inspired in exactly the same way as attacks upon the infant United States were inspired, two centuries ago, by those who have vested interest which they see imperilled by the establishment of political and economic freedom and by our efforts towards unity.

In exactly the same way as in the early days of the United States the Government was forced to take action in order to preserve itself against external and internal subversion, so we to-day have to exercise the utmost vigilance against those who would plan to overthrow our Constitution and to establish a Government not supported by popular will and mass enthusiasm.

I believe that the people of the United States should realise from their own historical experience, the problems with which we have to contend. We wish to do what they achieved so successfully in the early stages of their history. Within ten years of the Declaration of Independence, it was realised by the American people that though individual colonies had established their political independence, nevertheless they could not be really independent unless they were politically and economically united. The struggle to achieve this union was opposed not only by external and internal interests who hoped to profit financially from the disunity of the new world, but also by many individuals whom it can be seen mistakenly believed that freedom and justice could only be maintained by keeping intact the old colonial frontiers and by rejecting an effective form of union. It would indeed be a profound tragedy if the attacks of a prejudiced press and a misunderstanding of what we are attempting to do led any section of opinion or any influential organisation in the United States to support or conspire with those who are intriguing against African unity and against the establishment of a regime from which all traces of colonialism are eliminated.

I should like once again to welcome this Exhibition to Ghana and to express the hope that it will not only provide the maximum enjoyment to all who see it, but will also strengthen the relations between the United States of America and the Republic of Ghana.

Ladies and Gentlemen, I have pleasure in declaring this National United States Small Industries Exhibition formally open.

FLOWER OF LEARNING (2)

AT HIS INSTALLATION AS FIRST CHANCELLOR OF THE KWAME NKRUMAH UNIVERSITY OF SCIENCE AND TECHNOLOGY, DURING THE INAUGURATION OF THE UNIVERSITY

November 29, 1961.

Chairman of the University Council, Distinguished Guests, Ladies and Gentlemen:

I am happy to accept this great honour of being the first Chancellor of this University of Science and Technology which bears my name.

It is a little more than ten years ago that the decision was taken to establish in Kumasi a college "for the purpose of providing for studies and training in research, in technology, science and arts." Today, this decision has materialised in the establishment of this magnificent university in the heart of this city of Kumasi, the city of Osei Tutu and the Golden Stool, in the capital and historic city of Ashanti. I hope that the people of Ghana, and particularly the men and women of this region, will give this university their fullest support and co-operation. The very spot on which this university stands is historic. Recent excavations have shown that this was probably the home of people of the New Stone Age who skillfully adapted stone to all forms and shapes necessary for their existence in those harsh and difficult days. I have no doubt that this discovery may in some way be linked with the human-looking rock formations near Fomfompoom in Akitchiwe in the Central Region. I trust that students of geology and archaeology, and other scholars of our universities, will initiate research into these forms. Here we have a pointer to the role which this university is called upon to play in our modern society.

Modern life has become so complex that we can no longer rely on the stone implements and simple tools which were adequate for the needs of our ancestors. In a sense we must move swiftly from the stone age to the age of the atom. What it has taken other peoples and nations centuries to achieve, we have to carry out in a decade or generation. This places a heavy burden of responsibility on this university as a centre of science and technological education. It is only by a revolution of the political and social order, complete mental emancipation and the education of the miseducated, that we can achieve this rapid transformation.

Ghana has embarked on an industrial and agricultural revolution and initiated a programme of major industrial development designed to provide the basis of our progress and prosperity, and to sustain our ability to contribute to the advancement of the African continent. Only in this way can we keep pace with the swift scientific and technological advancement achieved in the progressive countries of the world.

This university, therefore, has a unique opportunity for making a positive contribution to the development of Ghana by directing its attention not only to the production of graduates in engineering, architecture, building and town planning, but also by addressing itself to investigation and research into the problems of industrialisation and agricultural development.

The Kumasi College of Technology occupied a very important place in the First Development Plan of the Government. In its early years, this institution failed to fulfil the hopes and aspirations of the nation. This may have been due to a lack of clear interpretation of its purpose and functions.

Fortunately, this university has emerged from the difficulties of its past into an era of confidence, purpose and power, and the nation can rely on it with faith and hope in the future.

It is a appropriate at this junction that I should enlarge on what the nation expects of our universities. A university must cultivate in its students a sound intellectual discipline and a keen sense of responsibility. It should give them training in their special fields as well as general educational background which should enable them to play their parts effectively as responsible and reliable citizens in a new evolving state.

Because this university is an institution for training in science and technology, it must use the facilities it possesses for research into fundamental problems as well as producing a body of men and women with sufficient scientific ability to apply the result of such research to the solution of immediate and practical problems.

Great responsibilities rest upon our shoulders as we inaugurate this university to-day. The measure of these responsibilities was clearly summarised in the report of the International Commission on University Education which I appointed in December, 1960. In view of its importance and significance, I quote again, as I did in may address at the University of Ghana last Saturday:

"In the effort to achieve these objectives the universities would be confronted with a two-fold task. On the one hand they are bound to be responsive to the sense of urgency that exists in a developing nation; to use their resources imaginatively and effectively to contribute to the economic and social progress; to interpret their studies for the benefit of the people and to learn from their problems."

Knowledge is international, and scientific knowledge especially cannot be restricted to any one particular nation. In other words, science knows no frontiers. It will therefore be the task of this university to enter into friendly association with other universities in Africa and outside the continent in furtherance of closer understanding between the nations. It must make a practical contribution to the political and economic unification of Africa.

The whole nation looks to this University of Science and Technology for inspiration and expects that from here will come the scientists and technologist upon whom Ghana and Africa will depend for progress and development.

In the distant past, universities were almost isolated from the life of a nation. But in this age, this is neither desirable nor possible. In our time, universities are looked upon almost as if they were the heart of the nation, essential to its life and progress. The very meaning of the word "academic" has changed. It no longer has the connotation of the abstract and sterile, for the academic has become both the functionary and the seer. The ivory tower concept of the university is dead (and may it rest in peace!)

Africa is changing fast; faster than in any other period of its history. It is because the rate of change in Africa is so much greater than at any other place at any time in the world's history, that our need for planned and co-ordinated development in agriculture and industry is so essential.

The adequate supply of food is an obvious requirement in any community. If manpower is to be made available for other activities to further the development of the county, the agricultural productivity must be increased by the introduction of new and scientific methods. For example, it will be necessary to introduce automation in order to accomplish a greater volume of work. It is one of the tasks of this university to supply agriculturalists who will go out and assist and advise our farmers and peasants. The introduction of new crops and new animal husbandry will assist in the diversification of the country's economy. The effective control of disease in both plants and livestock is another question of major importance. At the same time, our graduates must take with them a knowledge and understanding of indigenous methods of agriculture so that the innovations they suggest are really suited to the local situation. In addition to our immediate agricultural needs here in Ghana, there are vast areas in many parts of Africa in which it should be possible to return infertile land to production. The future scientists of Africa must make our deserts bloom. Where one blade of grass grew before, they must make two blades grow.

In order to transform Ghana into a modern industrial state, the first requirement is the development of sources of power. It is for this purpose that the Government has embarked on the Volta River scheme. There is little doubt that many of the students who are present here today will make great contributions towards this project.

I understand that there is under consideration here a scheme for the development of the Wiwi stream, which runs through the university, for the production of hydro-electric power. This scheme, which has been initiated by the university authorities, will when carried through, be of immense benefit not only to the university and the teaching of our future agriculturists, town planners and engineers, but also the whole of Kumasi and this region.

However, whilst it is true that the vast production of power in the one place is of great value, and that electrical power can be distributed to other parts of the country, there is also a need for other sources of energy. Fossil fuels are of limited use in Ghana as they have to be imported. The most important other sources of power in the world are from atomic reactors, and Ghanaians will soon share in the work and responsibilities of using modern reactors. There are other intriguing possibilities. The harnessing of energy from the sun has been the object of enquiry for centuries. Until recently the most efficient method of collecting solar energy has been the growth of timber which could then be burnt as fuel. There are now new devices made from semi-conductors which take the heat radiated from the sun and transform it directly into electricity. Elementary forms of water heating and cooking directly from solar energy have already been produced in many parts of the world, and their suitability under climatic conditions in Ghana has yet to be investigated. Not only do the methods of collecting useful energy require immediate study, but there is also the question of the storage of power. The adaptation of these devices in the use of solar energy have still to be investigated.

In addition to assistance in agriculture and power development with its consequent industrialisation, we are also much concerned with methods of transport and communication. In the past, African communication has looked outward. Our communications have stretched outwards to Europe instead of developing between our own cities and states. For example we can only speak to our brothers in Tunis by way of Paris. This must be changed, Africa must now look inward. Our engineers must be able to construct first-class highways, railroads and waterways to connect not only city to city, but state with state.

Africa has a potential hydraulic power unequalled by any continent and it is true to say that not even one-quarter per cent of this potential has been tapped. Imagine the industrial and agricultural advancement which would follow were all these sources of power developed to their fullest extent in the hands of a continental government of Africa. Our aeroplanes must fly across the continent from one terminus to the other. In short, African engineers must develop revolutionary methods of transport which can bind the whole continent into one unit, compact in thought and action.

In order to design and use this and other modern revolutionary forms of transport, we need mechanical engineers of highest quality. In addition, we must produce engineers with experience in communication so that the countries of Africa can be brought closer together.

Let us hope that from this university we can send out experts who will construct modern communication networks within Ghana and across the whole continent. Already the establishment of radio links between this country and our brothers in Guinea and Mali has been of the utmost importance. The presence of our troops assisting United Nations operations in the Congo has been greatly strengthened by constant direct wireless contact. The increasing ease with which one can speak to someone on the other side of Africa gives practical expression to the essential unity of our continent.

This university must seek to serve the needs of all our people. We need houses which are designed for our climate and which can be built economically. We need ready supplies of drugs for the sick; strong but simple bridges to make our villages more accessible; economic refrigeration units for the storage of food in our homes; measurement of earthquake tremors, and the design of buildings which will be safe for those who use them.

All these requirements will press heavily on this university and the nation will require both men and women equipped technically and morally to face with confidence these new horizons, men and women who have courage to face the future and who are not unconscious of the value of past experience. It is from this university in particular that the national needs will be met, and on it much of the future of this country and, possibly, of Africa will depend.

As your Chancellor I will take the greatest interest in the progress and development of this university. You can rely on my whole-hearted and unqualified support. Your tasks will be great and onerous. But I am sure that you, Mr. Vice Chancellor, as well as all the professors, lecturers and students, will fulfil these tasks with unflinching loyalty and devotion to the cause of truth and in the service of the nation.

We are determined that the pursuit of science in this university shall be positively assisted by conscious national measures designed to provide general preliminary preparation in scientific study. In this connection, science subjects will begin to be taught very early. From the upper classes of or middle schools science right up to the time they enter this university. Laboratories will be constructed in all these schools so that the time a child goes to the secondary school his interest in science must have been sufficiently aroused.

Everything will be done to place a premium on the study of science and technology. If need be, science subjects will become compulsory, and in any case the Party and the Government will make sure that every attraction necessary to induce the study of science is created without reserve.

Let me emphasise once more that the diversification and mechanisation of our agriculture, the intensive industrialisation of Ghana, all depend on the production of eminent scientists, technologist and technicians; indeed, the modern race for progress will be decisively won by the nation of dedicated scientists, and Ghana cannot afford to be left behind in this keen contest.

To expedite the training of tradesmen and technicians so essential to the development of the country, it may be necessary to link up all apprenticeship schemes and technical schools of the country to this university.

We must make science our pet subject and ensure that the very highest degree of creative intelligence and thought is sustained by the nation at all times.

Mr. Chairman, Ladies and Gentlemen, I have great pleasure in unveiling the plaque to mark the occasion of this university's formal inauguration. I am confident that in this university the nation has a sound foundation for progress in science and technology, for the prosperity and well-being of our people, and for the service of the nation.

23

CHRISTMAS BROADCAST

December 22, 1961

GOOD EVENING,

As 1961 draws to a close I should like to talk to you, my fellow citizens, about our national aspirations and hopes, and the progress we have made in consolidating our independence.

I have told you on many occasions of the basic goals which we have set before us in Ghana. We want to establish a happy society where men and women of all races can live together in peace and security; where hunger, unemployment, poverty and illiteracy no longer exist; where people are well housed; where our educational facilities will give our children every opportunity for learning; where every person can use his talents to the full and contribute to the general well being of our nation.

We cannot achieve any of these objectives, however, unless we are hardworking, disciplined and law-abiding. We only have to look to other parts of the world where the failure of Governments in this basic responsibility has led to human suffering and needless lose of lives. We must be careful to ensure that this does not happen here.

The Government of Ghana has had to deal recently with subversive acts and plots to overthrow our constitution by illegal means. It was necessary to deal with this dangerous situation swiftly and decisively in the interests of law and order. Our actions have been criticised, but I am sure that any Government faced with problems similar to our own would undoubtedly have taken similar action. The story of the circumstances which led to the Government's action against the recent conspiracy have already been published and known to you all. What I want to make quite clear is that my Government intends to preserve the rights and freedom of our people so long as these are exercised within the limits of the law and without threat to the safety and security of the nation. The Government and people of Ghana attached the same values and human rights, freedom and dignity that all peoples do throughout the world. We welcome criticism, but what we shall not tolerate is subversion against the state and illegal acts designed to promote the selfish interests of a minority. We have been able to achieve much in 1961. More schools and hospitals have been built and we have established our own universities where our scholars can have access to the highest opportunities for learning in our own environment. More houses have been built and more basic services such as roads, power and water have been provided in many parts of the country. All these developments will provide a better life for our people.

The Armed Services—that is, the army, the navy and air force, are being expanded. The police force has been strengthened. The Black Star Shipping Line and the Ghana Airways have expanded their operations. The great new harbour at Tema has been virtually completed, and Accra airport is rapidly being developed to a high international standard.

We have been active in all fields of agriculture. We have paid special attention to cocoa which for the present is our lifeblood. I have been greatly impressed with the improvement in our fishing industry which has been achieved both by the introduction of outboard motors on canoes and by the beginnings of intensive trawler operations. Much more can be done to diversify and mechanise our agriculture and we intend to do so.

Mining has been carried out successfully and we are intensifying geological surveys throughout the country. I am glad to say that the gold mines which the Government purchased early this year have operated successfully.

I am determined that our programme for industrialising Ghana should continue. In addition to those industries already established by the Government and by private investment, the Government intends to establish many other new industries. The foundations for the effective and rapid industrialisation of Ghana must rest on the provision of cheap and abundant power. Here, we must look to the Volta and our other rivers. The key to this is the great power development from the Volta at Akosombo and it is primarily about this project that I wish to speak to you tonight.

Before talking of the project itself, I want to pay a particular tribute to President Kennedy and the United States Government. The personal interest shown by the President in this vast project is great deal to me personally and to the people of Ghana. The project is another example of a growing number of instances where the goals and objectives of our two governments harmonise. This combined effort will doubtless strengthen the good will and friendship between our two countries and contribute generally to the well being of the United States and Ghana. The co-operation also demonstrate the awareness of the United States of the problems and aspirations of modern Africa.

After ten years unceasing effort, we have at last succeeded in getting this great scheme under way. We have obtained the necessary financial resources for its construction, and we have reached agreement with the Volta Aluminum Company for the establishment of a large smelter at Tema.

As the project now stands, I believe that it will be the largest single integrated scheme in Africa. By any international standards, it will represent one of the largest single investments in the world. Great sums of money are involved. We in Ghana who have always believed in this great national undertaking have from our own resources already invested nearly £G30 million in the construction of the new port at Tema which is an integral part of the Volta River Project. Essential roads and preliminary works at Akosombo and the new township at Tema have also been constructed from our own resources. We shall need to provide another £G35 million for our share, which is half of the total cost of the dam and hydro-electric installation and the transmission lines which will carry power to other parts of Ghana. We are thus investing a great deal of our country's resources in this scheme. These facts are not always sufficiently appreciated by those foreign critics who say that we have frittered away our reserves. I hope, indeed, that our other partners will regard our efforts as a clear proof of our determination to make the whole project a success.

Thomas Jefferson, a great American, stated what defines more clearly my conception of alignment. In his inaugural address some 170 years ago, he said in connection with American foreign policy:

"Peace, commerce and honest friendship with all nations—entangling alliances with none."

It is exactly in this same spirit that Ghana has accepted loans towards the Volta River Project, amounting to £G17 million from the International Bank of Reconstruction and Development; £G5 million from the United Kingdom Government; £G13 million from the United States Government. We look upon our acceptance of these loans and the negotiations that we have carried out with the Soviet Union for the development of power from the Bui, as a practical demonstration of our policy of non-alignment in action. Thus it is not primarily the financial value of the loans which is important. The important point is that it is possible for a developing country to enter into financial and commercial relations of such magnitude with foreign powers without in the least effecting its independence of thought and action.

Before developing this aspect of the matter, I would like to make one or two observations. First let me emphasise that the loans being provided from abroad are not free grants or gifts. They are commercial loans upon which we must pay interest.

I must emphasise that ultimately Ghana will have to find every single penny we shall spend on the Volta scheme together with the interest which we must pay on the money which has been lent to us. Indeed, it is our misfortune that we shall have to borrow the money which we require at a far higher rate of interest than we ourselves secured when our own financial reserves were invested on our behalf.

The offer of these loans from the United States and the United Kingdom is, however, a genuine endeavour in which two of the most advanced and wealthiest countries of the world will be working in partnership with us on a basis of mutual understanding and complete equality. The United States Government's interest in the Volta scheme goes even further than their loan to the Ghana Government of £G13 million. They have also lent to a consortium of American aluminum companies about £G45 million in order to enable this group, which has formed a Ghanaian company known as *VALCO*, to erect a smelter in Ghana. This company, which is itself investing about £G15 million in the smelter, is prepared to enter into a thirty-year contract for the purchase of electric power from the Volta dam as soon as it is completed. The initial investment of £G60 million will in fact rise to about £G100 million as the smelter is developed to full capacity. This demonstrates how vital the smelter is to the Volta project as a whole, and it will be seen that the resources provided by the United States Government and the American companies are therefore of the greatest help to Ghana.

However, in spite of such assistance from abroad, it is imperative that we should so order our national economy that we can repay the interest and principal on the loans which we have obtained. In five years time when the dam is completed, there will be an abundance of electricity. Our factories must therefore be ready to use this power as soon as it becomes available.

How are we going to pay for such factories? In the western world when industrialisation started there were many wealthy men ready to invest in new inventions and in new industries. Such a monied class does not exist in Ghana. If, therefore, we are to use the electricity which we shall soon have, we have three courses open to us. We may be able to find some foreign investors from foreign countries who are willing to invest in industry in Ghana. We shall, of course, welcome such investment. Private foreign investment from abroad is, however, open to a number of objections. First, the private investor naturally wishes to make large a profit as possible and the types of industry and trade in which the largest profits can be made are not necessarily the ones which would serve the interests of Ghana. What we require are industries which will build up our export trade, diminish our need for foreign imports and employ as many of our people as possible, thus increasing the prosperity of our country.

Secondly, the foreign investors naturally wishes to export as much of his profit as possible to his own home country. Our interest is that profit from industry should be ploughed back into Ghana so as to develop further industry. Finally, if we rely exclusively or even largely upon private foreign investment for our industrialisation, we would in fact become politically and economically dependent upon expatriate interests. Indeed all we should be doing would be to reintroduce colonialism in another guise. While, therefore, private foreign investment can play a useful and valuable part in the development of the country, we cannot expect it to play a major role.

The second method by which our industrialisation can be financed is by way of foreign loans and credits. For this purpose, credits have been obtained from the Soviet Union, China, and countries in eastern Europe including Yugoslavia, Poland, Czechoslovakia, Bulgaria, Rumania, the German Democratic Republic and Hungary, amounting to no less than £100 million sterling. Such loans and credits are of great assistance to us but, whether they come either from the east or the west, they do not ultimately provide us with capital. They merely postpone the time when we have to pay for our new industries. In other words, we do not have to repay such credit until the project which it is used to establish is working satisfactorily. It is important therefore that we spent such loans on projects which will be remunerative and which, by the profits they make, will enable us to pay off the loans as quickly as possible.

It would be absurdly optimistic that we can secure through foreign loans sufficient funds to finance our own developments. The Volta scheme, for which foreign loans of £30 million are now at last available, has taken nearly ten years to negotiate. If we had not been able to construct the Tema harbour out of our own resources, we should never even have been able to obtain the loan of £30 million. required for the major project.

The lesson of the Volta negotiations is that we must in the future depend upon our own resources in order to build the industries we shall require. Our task now is to make the Volta River Project a success. To achieve success, we will need good men to build the project and I am confident that the consortium of contractors at Akosombo, *IMPREGILO*, and our consulting engineers, Kaiser, will do first class work. Our own Ghanaians have already demonstrated, on projects such as the new port at Tema, what they can do, and I am certain that they will produce still more impressive results at Akosombo.

But, as I have said, men can only work well if there is internal peace and stability. Therefore the Government will continue to preserve and maintain stability in the country. Political and civil rights of all Ghanaian citizens will be strictly upheld. But this does not mean that a few people will be allowed to abuse and misuse these rights to jeopardise the security and sovereignty of our state.

Similarly we are determined to ensure that the best possible use is made of our own money and the loans from overseas. We therefore have an equally strong interest in preserving financial and economic stability. The Budget introduced last July was an important step in attaining this basic objective. Since then we have established central economic planning machinery, and introduced physical control over imports and exports. The Government will take such further action as may be necessary, including the channelling of credit in such a manner as to preserve and increase our economic strength, and to give priority to development, agriculture and industry.

Another aspect of the project is the great smelter at Tema, for the smelter company VALCO, by paying for the power generated at Akosombo, will do much to repay the great investment in the hydroelectric scheme. A large sum of money will be invested in this smelter, and we have guaranteed it against expropriation for the first thirty years of its operation. I do not think that overseas firms need entertain any fear in this respect.

When talking about the Volta River, I also wish to mention the fact that with the assistance of the Government of the Soviet Union, we are surveying the power potential at Bui, and with the help of the Government of Czechoslovakia, we are investigating the possibilities of generating power from other rivers in the Western Region. Investigations are also being carried out into the possibilities of developing our mineral resources throughout the country.

We are embarking on the Volta River Project at a time when I am certain that the Government can maintain the necessary political and economic stability to ensure the success of the project. However, I am very conscious of the difficult and dangerous situation which exists in the world as a whole, and it is for that reason that the Government of Ghana has genuinely followed a policy of independence and non-alignment. I have said again and again that this does not mean a neutral attitude to our relations with the rest of the world.

What it means is that we shall maintain the courage of our convictions and shall judge every political problem on its merits, and adopt whatever policy or measure we believe will do most to safeguard our own independence and further our national interest. In the past all our economic links were with the countries of the west. It is natural, and in keeping with our policy of independence and non-alignment, to create new links with other countries such as Russia, China and those in eastern Europe.

The fact that we have established these new relations and our insistence on unity in Africa, have aroused much comment in some western countries, and our policy of non-alignment has been questioned. In deciding which is the best way to organise the political and economic life of our country we shall continue to study what is done in other countries and try to profit by their experience. We can, however, only successfully use the experience of other countries if we do this with due regard to our own indigenous political and economic institutions and our way of life. We must adopt a socialist method of achieving our agricultural and industrial expansion, but this does not mean that we shall blindly follow the methods of socialism adopted in other places.

As an example of our desire to profit by the best experience available in the west and in the east, I hope that the World Bank will accept my invitation to send to Accra a resident financial expert who can consult with us in regard to our international financial transactions. This however, does not mean that the World Bank will dictate our financial policy, any more than our socialist policy will be dictated by any particular socialist country. Non-alignment means that we seek advice and help from all, but direction or dictation from none. We, and we alone, are the masters of our fate and destiny. Any objective and impartial examination of our record and our policies will show that we have not departed from our non-alignment policy. And why should we? We have no desire to become part of the cold war, or to create conditions to imperil our hard-won independence. We welcome close working relations with the west and east, so long as our national sovereignty is fully safeguarded.

My views on pan-Africanism are well known. On the eve of independence, I declared to the world that the independence of

Ghana was meaningless unless it was linked up with the total liberation of Africa. The number of countries that have become independent in Africa since then shows how right our policy has been. The burning desire of the African peoples all over the continent for human rights, for dignity and for independence, has never been so manifest as in the past few years. We shall continue to wage a relentless war against colonialism and neo-colonialism in Africa, and we shall not rest until every inch of African territory is free and Africa is united.

These are the goals which we seek. We hope that visitors from other parts of the world will come and see for themselves what we are trying to achieve in our country.

Nineteen sixty-one brought many distinguished visitors to Ghana, including several Heads of State and Heads of Government.

It is true to say that all these distinguished leaders were impressed with what they saw in our country, and with the warmth of the welcome extended to them. It has therefore been a great surprise to me that the image of Ghana in certain countries abroad has been so badly and deliberately distorted and misrepresented by a section of the Press in those countries. Writers, journalists, statesmen, scholars, radio and television representatives will always be welcome in Ghana, All that we ask is that they should report honestly and accurately, and avoid sensationalism, ill-founded speculation or deliberate distortion which can do such great harm to relations between their countries and our own. I wonder sometimes whether the Press as a whole fully appreciates its enormous responsibility in this age of fear and suspicion, an age in which we all live from day to day in peril of atomic annihilation. The power of the Press to do good is immense, but its power to arouse the worst emotions in man is even greater. To a special degree, we in Ghana have been conscious of this power to choose between good and evil.

And now, as we enter into the New Year, I wish to call upon you all to rededicate yourselves to the service of Ghana and the cause of African unity. For Christians, Christmas is of profound significance and with them, and with people of all other religious beliefs and creeds, I join in the eternal appeal for peace on earth, goodwill and friendship among the nations of the world.

I wish you all a merry Christmas and happiness in the coming year.

Good night.

24

A CHRISTMAS TOAST AT A DINNER FOR AMBASSADORS AND MINISTERS

December 22, 1961

LADIES AND GENTLEMEN,

We have arrived at the time of the year when a large proportion of mankind makes a determined effort to be nice to their fellow men. Suddenly this topsy-turvey world seems rather a wonderful place to live in. Debtors cease to be hounded by their creditors, and quarrels are patched up. The cost of living, nuclear weapons and even party politics become matters of secondary importance.

A great change comes over man. He forgets himself and his worries. He is suddenly seized by a frantic urge to do good to others and instead of saying "What can I GET?" he says "What can I GIVE?" Each year, when this happens to him, he discovers anew, with the same thrill and freshness as though he had never experienced it all before, the great joy and happiness that he derives from doing all this good.

Well—no matter whether we are Christians or not, we really cannot help but be grateful for Christmas. For, if Christmas can achieve this miracle of love and goodwill among so many different types of men—even if it only lasts for such a regrettably short period in each year—then, surely it deserves to be encouraged and celebrated. It is an excellent thing that such an opportunity should be regularly afforded man to escape temporarily from the rut of selfishness, aggressiveness and other anti-social and unpleasant habits that usually make up his daily life. And, if we are somewhat disappointed that this upsurge of loving-kindness and good works—to say nothing of those well-mentioned New Year resolutions!—rarely survive the first few days of January—take heart!—for as sure as nothing follows day, it will all come back again in full measure next December!

Whether we are Christians or not, we should be glad to associate ourselves with the flow of good cheer that Christmas brings. Those of us here tonight are representatives of many different nations with different outlooks and different creeds. And yet I am sure I am right in saying that there is not one of us who is not caught up in this whirlwind of goodwill. We all sincerely desire peace and friendship with every one around us and feel down in our hearts, the desire to do as much as we can to foster such noble sentiments.

Very shortly we will enter into the New Year. A fresh start is offered to us, a chance to take stock of ourselves, to sift the good things about us from the less desirable things, our successes from our failures. We will start off with a large credit balance of good intentions.

In spite of the old saying—"The road to hell is paved with good intentions," I think that it is better to start the New Year with good intentions than with nothing at all. One thing that we tend to overlook is that goodwill, peace and friendship require an equal amount of give and take, and sincerity on both sides. Maybe we are too proud sometimes or too sensitive to pour out our hearts; instead, we hold back our innermost and best feelings or stifle them with so much pride that they go unrecognised.

I feel that mankind can do well in the coming year to do some serious soul-searching. I think every man and woman, every leader, every nation, should ask themselves this questions: "Do I honestly desire peace and friendship throughout the world?"

If the answer is sincerely in the affirmative, then we must bend our wills, and concentrate our energies on working to bring this about

It has given me a great deal of pleasure to entertain you all tonight. I shall see to it—and this is not just an empty New Year resolution—that we have such dinners regularly year by year.

And now, Ladies and Gentlemen, I would like to propose a toast: To goodwill, to friendship and to peace among the nations and throughout the world.

25

SEASON OF GOODWILL

NEW YEAR'S EVE BROADCAST
December 31, 1961

GOOD EVENING,

In a few hours, the canons will boom, the bells will toll, 1961 will come to an end, and we shall usher in the New Year. I have therefore come to the studio tonight to share with you a few thoughts on our national life. In my Christmas message last week, I dwelt mainly on the many things which the Party and the Government are doing to bring about material progress and to provide a better life for us all. Silently, but steadily, an industrial, scientific, and agricultural revolution is taking place in Ghana which, in a few years time, should make it a developed and industrialised country. At the same time, though less obvious, a social revolution is taking place which is even more challenging.

I sometimes wonder, however, whether the masses of our people appreciate sufficiently the full significance of these changes. We are tempted, I think, to take it all for granted, and fail to realise that each one of us must make a positive and constructive contribution to the changes now taking place around us.

I am speaking now to all of you, both Ghanaians and our friends from overseas who are working here with us. All of us, whether we be carpenters, doctors, shop-keepers, market women, lawyers, messengers, clerks, civil servants, farmers, ministers of state or labourers, owe a duty to the state, and no sacrifice should be too great to carry it out. I am sure that each one of us in our own way can contribute to the happiness and welfare of the community. The positions which we hold are in themselves only a means to an end, namely, service of the community and the state. We must not use our positions, therefore, for the gratification of ourselves at the expense of our fellow citizens. We should say to ourselves honestly and convincingly, and repeat it time and again: "I hold this position irrespective of any remuneration or glory that I may receive on account of it; I will use it only to make Ghana great, prosperous and universally respected."

And so, I particularly want to speak to you tonight about our responsibility to our fellow men and to the state. I want to do this because unless we are very careful, we are in danger of losing the sense of brotherhood, team spirit and fellowship which has been the essential feature of our society, and which is the basis of African humanism. I am speaking to you now not so much as the President of Ghana, your President, but rather as fellow Ghanaian who is concerned not only about the material development of his country and its people, but also about our spiritual, moral and cultural well-being.

I have referred to the sense of brotherhood and fellowship which is the basis of African humanism. This humanism is revealed daily in every African family, village and community. Whoever you are, and wherever you are this evening, you understand perfectly well what I am saying. When children are born, when people are named, when people are indisposed and when people die, we all show our concern and obligation. We give the present to the child's parents or to the married couple, or to the sick or to the family of the dead. This we have always done: we share our joys and sorrows alike.

Again, we have always lived together and helped one another and the community generally—by communal labour. As we built our houses, as we cleared the roads and paths, as we dug wells for water or put out a fire, or, with the drum searched for a missing brother, relative or friend, or marshalled our men for action, we were discharging our obligations heartily and joyfully to the community and the state.

This spontaneous fellow-feeling, this sense of obligation and the belief that we are our brother's keeper, has held us together and preserved our solidarity and integrity. It constitutes the material, moral, spiritual and cultural bedrock of our communal life.

These are some of the things to which, I think, we should give serious thought as we enter the New Year. We must bring ourselves to order, for our way of life in Ghana has stood the test of time and is appreciated everywhere.

In recent times, we seem to be departing very seriously from these simple but precious virtues which have held our society together and strengthened it. New developments in Ghana have brought in their wake vast opportunities for the advancement of the individual, and many of you today are in positions of great responsibility and authority undreamt of a few years ago. You must remember, therefore that you have equally great obligations to society and to your state.

Unfortunately, there are too many instances where people hold their positions too lightly, with arrogance, egotism, and without humility, have betrayed the trust reposed in them and indulged in vanity and self-gratification. If we do not avoid these pitfalls here and now, we shall be heading towards spiritual, moral and cultural confusion and bankruptcy which could defeat the purpose of our endeavours.

Now, fellow Ghanaians: the building of a modern state and the development of the country—in effect, the fight against insecurity, disease, poverty, hunger, unemployment, illiteracy and ignorance, the fight for good, clothing and shelter are, as you know, our present preoccupations.

Countrymen:

Industries are springing up and transforming simple communities into urban societies. In the wake of this necessary transformation are many dangers and pitfalls which threaten our values, complicate our obligations and responsibilities, confuse our thinking and place many temptations in our way. I know that there are many of you who still keep these simple virtues, who toil away quietly and tirelessly for the good of the state and of your fellow citizens. I hope that your example will be a light to others.

We have a record in Ghana of hospitality, racial tolerance and friendliness of spirit, which does not fail to evoke the admiration of foreign visitors. This is a valuable national asset which we must strive to maintain.

We have in our midst many devoted loyal workers from other countries who have identified themselves with our cause. These men and women have left homes and friends to come to work among us. There are many others whom we have invited here to assist us to develop our country. The help they are able to give us is the best that can be obtained anywhere in the world, for they are specialists in their own fields. But whether they have come here of their own accord or at our invitation, they have remained here because of the happy atmosphere which they find here. Many of them genuinely and sincerely desire the progress of Ghana. Those who have such a spirit deserve our co-operation and support in all they do for the good of the nation, and we should do nothing to discourage them.

As I had occasion to say recently, Ghana and Africa need "a new type of man: a dedicated, modest, honest and devoted man. A man who submerges himself in service to his nation and mankind. A man who abhors greed and detests vanity. A new type of man whose meekness is his strength and whose integrity is his greatness."

You can transform yourself into this type of man now. Why don't you resolve to do so as you enter the New Year?

I have often marvelled at the way ants store their food and I have been astonished at their sense of discipline and devotion as they go about their duties in building their anthills. What an example to us, too, is the sense of belonging to the community which the honey bees display in manufacturing and storing their honey. What discipline! What patience! What devotion!

Unhappily, some of us these days want big jobs and fat salaries when we have no intention to do any serious work. If we don't get what we want, we lose interest and say: "Well if I can't be this or that, why should I bother? Country broke or country no broke, we dey." But why should the country become "broke" if you are there to help it?

I must confess to you, however, that as I speak to you now, I am overwhelmed with a keen sense of pride and gratitude—pride in the quality of our human make-up which causes us to radiate so much warmth—warmth of sincere and genuine affection for our friends, our guests and the strangers within our gates. Let us treasure this human quality which makes our Ghanaian hospitality so proverbial.

But the pride and gratitude which I feel at the moment stems from a different source. I am grateful to all of you, not only for your devotion and loyalty to me personally and to my office, to the Party and the Government, but also for the fact that you understand so well the great cause for which I personally stand, that is to say, the rediscovery of African self-respect and dignity, and the unity and solidarity of Africa.

Let us go into the New Year with hope and confidence, with a will to work and a determination to serve one another in our country.

I wish every one of you a happy and prosperous New Year.

www.ingramcontent.com/pod-product-compliance
Lightning Source LLC
Chambersburg PA
CBHW021830300426
44114CB00009BA/391